CODEPENDENCY

STOP CONTROLLING OTHERS AND BOOST YOUR SELF-ESTEEM. HOW TO SPOT AND SURVIVE THE HIDDEN GASLIGHT EFFECT, SAVE RELATIONSHIPS AFFECTED BY ADDICTION, ABUSE, TRAUMA OR TOXIC SHAMING

D1718895

Table of Contents

Introduction... 1

Chapter 1 What is Codependency? 5

Chapter 2 Symptoms of Codependency..................................... 9

Chapter 3 Crossing De-Nile to Recovery 13

Chapter 4 So, Are You Codependent? 21

Chapter 5 Getting Started in Recovery.................................... 24

Chapter 6 What Made You Codependent? 29

Chapter 7 Healing Your Wounds — Freeing Your Self 34

Chapter 8 Welcome to the Real You....................................... 40

Chapter 9 Building Self-Esteem and Self-Love 49

Chapter 10 Finding Pleasure.. 53

Chapter 11 Letting Go and Non-attachment.......................... 68

Chapter 12 Speaking Up... 75

Chapter 13 Relating to Your Family, Friends, and Lovers 85

Chapter 14 Making Relationships Work.................................. 97

Chapter 15 Following Your Bliss 106

Chapter 16 The People-Pleaser 114

Chapter 17 Being Assertive.. 120

Chapter 18 The essential dictionary to understanding
narcissistic abuse 125

Conclusion 144

Introduction

Before you can put codependency completely behind you, you have to love, respect and come to terms with the real you. For so long, you have been trapped in a cycle of caring for others, putting them first, and denying your own true self. Now, take the time to get to know you and find the courage to love yourself for who you are.

Step One: Discover Who You Are As an Individual

People in codependent relationships commonly define themselves in terms of their relationships. They might be a caring wife, a good daughter, a loving mother or a faithful friend. All these roles can be important to you, but for now, think of who you are as a person apart from these roles.

Get out your journal again and make a list of the things you like. Write down the things that make you happy and the things that make you sad. Mention activities and events you enjoy.

Then, write down the things that make you different from other people. Avoid judging yourself as you think of these things. Also, keep to those things that are unique to you as a person rather than you as a member of a relationship.

Step Two: Accept Who You Are Not

Perhaps you have buried the real you to protect yourself or to take care of your partner's needs. You do things you do not like to do, just as everyone must at some time in their life. The difference in a codependent relationship is that you lose sight of your distaste for the role, the activity or the conversations. You become the role, despite the fact that it causes you to put aside what benefits you.

So, spend some time thinking about things, people, thoughts, behaviors and emotions that you do not identify with or want to include in your life. You have probably already realized that you do not like your partner's addictions. Yet there is more to who you are than that one issue.

Write down those things you disagree with or do not enjoy in your daily life. Write down activities or events you would not want to participate in. Write down the names of people you do not want to be part of your life.

Step Three: Realize Your Limitations

Take the concept of what you are not a step further and think about what your limitations are, both in the codependent relationship and in other parts of your life. For instance, you do not have the power to end your partner's addiction. You cannot get inside your partner's mind and figure out what will change his behavior. You are not physically strong enough to withstand constant physical abuse without injury or pain. In short, you are not superhuman.

Aside from these limitations, shared by all humans, you have other more personal limitations. Is there a limit to your capacity to help your partner? Is there a limit to your patience? Write down some examples of things you cannot do that others can. Realize that you can become stronger, but you will always have limitations. Everyone does.

Step Four: Look for Your Strengths

Now, look for your strengths. Your first reaction as someone who struggles with codependency issues might be your caretaking ability. Set that aside for now and think about your other positive qualities. Think about the things you are good at now and those you excelled in during your childhood. Consider the positive values you adhere to and that make you different from other people. Make a list of the great things that make you who you are.

Step Five: Explore Your Needs for Personal Growth

As you contemplate your weaknesses and limitations, it is common to feel bad about yourself and judge yourself harshly. Understand and remember that criticizing yourself has no value and is a total waste of time. Instead, take your personal weaknesses as indications of issues where you can improve. Write down some things you want to do, skills you want to develop and qualities you want to magnify in yourself. Then, start taking steps to make those self-improvements.

Step Six: Express Your Self Respect

Once you have a solid sense of who you are and what you want out of life, express those thoughts, needs and wants assertively and often. The more you show your respect for you, the more your self-esteem improves. You are a good person regardless of what anyone, including your partner, might say or do. Allow yourself to feel good about who you are, and don't let fear stop you from telling the world.

Chapter 1 What is Codependency?

Being in a codependent relationship is much like taking a ride on a never-ending rollercoaster of emotion. It doesn't matter on which side of the codependency coin you are, whether you are a pleaser, a fixer, an addict, or a caregiver; one relies on the other for a complete sense of who they are.

The first step on the road to recovery from a codependent relationship is to understand what it means. Codependency, like several psychological concepts, can be highly confusing, but in simple terms is nothing but relationship addiction. It is a behavioral and psychological condition, where one individual is excessively reliant on another for their identity, self-worth and validation.

Some experts are of the view that it is an obsessive preoccupation with other people's problems in a bid to meet one's own neglected emotional needs; while others suggest codependency is an unhealthy pattern of excessive dependence on other people and their approval to find your identity. A third opinion is that codependency is a relationship condition where the real issue stems from an individual's lack of relationship with himself or herself.

A widely prevalent codependent definition suggests growing up being dependent on someone who in turn is dependent on an element that is non-dependable. It could be drugs, alcohol, overeating, or an excessive indulgence in sex –anything compulsive and overdone.

With all these differing and confusing definitions, it is no wonder codependency is so hard to understand. If you have read this far you might be thinking about how you ended up in a codependent relationship. Below I have listed the main ways codependency manifests.

Learnt Behavior

Observing older members in the family often teaches codependency. Children in homes where both partners share an unhealthy, destructive or abusive relationship are more prone to be a part of codependent relationships themselves. They observe, learn and invariably internalise the behaviour to display similar behaviour patterns in their future relationships as they move into adulthood.

Repressing an Issue Within A Relationship

Dysfunctional families breed codependency by their inability to acknowledge the existence of a problem. Underlying issues such as shame, anger, pain and jealously are often brushed under the carpet without being resolved. The issues can stem from addiction (alcohol, drugs, sex or gambling), abuse (mental, physical and sexual), or chronic mental or physical illness. Rather than talking about these issues or tackling them head on, there is a tendency to repress the core problem.

Addiction

The term codependent was initially used as synonym for enabler. Enablers 'helped' addicts with their highly compulsive tendencies by taking control of the situation and assuming personal responsibility for the addict; often by rationalising their behaviour, protecting them by making excuses, and covering up for their actions. Within a codependent relationship where one partner is an addict, there is tendency to deny the consequences of the addict's dysfunctional behavioural patterns, and although done with the very best of intention, does nothing but prolong the situation.

Codependency was a term first coined by Alcoholics Anonymous, and primarily centred on the problem of compulsive alcohol addiction, where the family and well meaning friends of the addict unwittingly encouraged and supported their addiction by enabling their dysfunctional behaviour.

Abuse

In an abusive relationship, the suffering family member stifles his emotions and disregards his own requirements to turn into some sort of 'survivor'. They get habituated to denying or ignoring tricky emotions. They don't communicate, detach themselves from the underlying issue and avoid confrontation, often shutting out others outside of the relationship. They begin to become an extension of the abuser, denouncing all thoughts

Putenfleisch	-10,5
Margarine	-7,5
Butter	-3,9
Steinpilze	+4,0
Pfifferlinge	+4,5

Früchte

Johannisbeeren (rot)	+2,4
Erdbeeren	+3,1
Birnen	+3,2
Kirschen (sauer)	+3,5
Apfel (reif)	+4,1
Kirschen (süß)	+4,4
Ananas	+4,6
Datteln	+4,7
Bananen (unreif)	+4,8
Mirabellen	+4,9
Zwetschgen	+4,9
Himbeeren	+5,1
Heidelbeeren	+5,3
Pflaumen	+5,8
Johannisbeeren (schwarz)	+6,1
Pfirsiche	+6,4
Aprikosen	+6,6
Preiselbeeren	+7,0
Brombeeren	+7,2
Trauben	+7,6
Stachelbeeren	+7,7
Korinthen	+8,2
Apfelsinen	+9,2
Zitronen	+9,9
Bananen (reif)	+10,1
Mandarinen	+11,5

Rosinen	+15,1
Hagebutten	+15,5
Feigen (getrocknet)	+27,5

Milch, Milcherzeugnisse

Hartkäse	-18,1
Quark	-17,3
Sahne	-3,9
H-Milch	-1,0
Buttermilch	+1,3
Ziegenmilch	+2,4
Molke	+2,6
Schafmilch	+3,2
Kuhmilch (Vorzugsmilch)	+4,5

Mehl, Teigwaren

Reis (geschält)	-39,1
Roggenmehl (Auszug)	-16,4
Graupen	-13,7
Reis (naturbelassen)	-12,5
Weizengrieß	-10,1
Haferflocken	-9,2
Nudeln (weiß)	-5,9
Grünkern	-4,6
Reisstärke	-4,6
Suppengrieß	-4,6
Buchweizengrütze	-3,7
Weizenmehl (Auszug)	-2,6
Nudeln (Vollkorn)	-2,0
Sojamehl	+12,8
Sojagranulat	+24,0
Soja-»Nüsse«	+26,5
Soja-Reinlecithin	+38,0

Brot, Zwieback

Schwarzbrot (Graubrot)	-17,0
Weißbrot	-10,0
Kommissbrot	-7,3
Zwieback (weiß)	-6,5
Schrotbrot	-6,1
Vollkornbrot	-6,0
Vollwertbrot	-4,5
Knäckebrot	-3,7
Zwieback (Vollkorn)	-2,2
Vollkornknäcke	-0,5
Dinkelbrot (alle Sorten)	+

Nüsse

Erdnüsse	-12,7
Paranüsse	-8,8
Walnüsse	-8,0
Mandeln (süß)	-0,6
Haselnüsse	-0,2

and feelings of their own and begin to base their sense of self-worth on what the abuser thinks of them. This lack of feelings and mistrust invariably leads to impaired psychological and identity development.

Mental Health/Physical Disability (the caring role)

In relationships where one person suffers from a mental health condition, or physical disability, another assumes the caring role. This can create a situation where the carer, takes control of everything on behalf of the other person, to the extent of preventing the person with the condition or disability from reaching their true potential. The carer will take over everything, often quite simple tasks that the other person could quite easily do for himself or herself. This will all be done in the name of caring, but in reality this is just another example of a codependent relationship, and similar to an abusive relationship, the other person learns to keep quiet and to accept what they are told without question.

Although the strategies you will find in the following chapters can be used with whatever codependent relationship you may find yourself in; for the purposes of this book, we will be primarily focusing on intimate relationships between two people.

Chapter 2 Symptoms of Codependency

Your mind and body operate as a "smart system" that is capable of evaluating for your needs and determining what you will need to do in order to meet those needs. You have built a library of activities and events that you use to help you meet your needs and your "smart system" evaluates and chooses what it believes to be the best option(s) in order to deal with whatever is happening at the moment.

Because no other person can live your life for you, it follows that if you are unhappy or uncertain or uneasy, then you are the only person on this planet who can do anything about it. No one else can do that for you. And, that is why it is important that you take full and complete responsibility for your life.

The rules that govern how your life plays out are:

1. Everything you do or have is the result of the choices you make.

2. You will always experience what you create (through your choices).

3. You can do anything you want, any time you want, anywhere you want, as long as you're willing to pay the price... without whining or blaming.

Our initial suggestions concerning making change is to address the topics of gratitude and responsibility:

1. by developing an "attitude of gratitude" you will find it much, much easier to overcome those beliefs that hold you back – we call them limiting beliefs. For those who feel they have little or nothing to be grateful for, we will show you how to assess and evaluate for the good things in your life.

2. by taking responsibility for every action you undertake – regardless of the hand you were dealt in life – you will not get lost in the "blame game" that defines victimhood.

WHAT? BE RESPONSIBLE FOR MY ACTIONS EVEN

WHEN THERE IS SOMEONE ELSE TO BLAME?

Absolutely. Blaming is a depressing and useless exercise that fixes nothing and is not a pretty thing to watch. However, if you do only those things that are in your own Best Interest you won't suffer from guilt, anxiety, inferiority, or even drinking, drugging or excessive eating in an attempt to "deal" with your problems. By taking responsibility for your own thoughts and actions you can learn to feel better about yourself. And, when that happens your Codependent behaviours will no longer be your "default" setting.

And that's a major win.

The point at which responsibility for self comes into your life is the point where you get to pick your own direction and discover what and who you want to be – and Dynamic Discovery will show you how to do just that.

Relationships

Relationships are a huge part of human life. We have relationships with people, places and things. Some are good (happy), some are bad (unhappy). The quality of your relationships is governed by your behaviours, meaning how you act. And how you act is based upon your values and beliefs, which may be at odds with those around you and would explain why you sometimes engage in conflict or are out of step with the rest of society.

Codependent relationships are typically derived from emotional and behavioural conditions that are often not satisfying and are sometimes unhealthy, one-sided, emotionally crippling, and abusive. This type of behavior is also known as "relationship addiction".

Now, this is not to say that so-called normal intimate relationships are all springtime and flowers, because they're not. Every intimate relationship has its ups and downs but that is not the issue here: Codependent persons are addicted to helping others and need to be needed. And, sometimes this need is so powerful that the other person becomes locked into being needy. Enabling is the word for this behavior.

This type of relationship may not be in your long-term Best Interest because it does not meet the definition whereby Best

Interest is defined as not being deliberately hurtful or harmful to yourself or anyone else.

Our process for self-evaluation will allow you to determine for yourself what to do in order to meet your "real" needs. Because no other person can live your life for you, it follows that you are the one person on this planet who can make the changes required so that you can get what you really, really, really want – happiness, or peace, or contentment, or calm. And, no one else can do that for you.

Please remember this: The human being is the only creature on earth that is not a prisoner of its programming but the master of it, and therefore no human needs to live with unhappiness, guilt, resentment, etc., for one more day because we have all been gifted with the ability to effect change.

Let that sink in...

You have been gifted with the ability to effect change. Change how you think and feel and change your life.

Chapter 3 Crossing De-Nile to Recovery

Often times all the above leads to dysfunction in marriages, this becomes the cause and effect of troubled parenthood and dysfunction in Family, on a whole. The troublesome marriages end up in a divorce or separation, for which the children bears the fruits.

Parenthood as a Co-dependency Parameter

Co-dependent Parents

Co-dependency of Fear in Parenthood is one of the most general occurrences of co-dependency in parenthood.

1.   Over consciousness: one of the effective stabilizing of a parent's co-dependency is through their acts from over-consciousness. As they are perpetually worried about their kids, they establish a argument that is paranoid, whenever the kid raises a topic.

2.   Holding authority over all personal decisions: is one category of parents, who tend to believe that they have the right to exert authority over all of their child's decisions, regardless of their importance.

3.   Over-bonding Parenthood: some parents try to bond too much to their kids by becoming the creepy or interfering element in their personal space, peace and calms that the kid grows up to be paranoid of everything in their life. For example, a kid hates anyone touching their stuff in a shared hotel room. This owes to the fact that her mom had a nosy habit of going through her personal belongings by utilizing the excuse of cleaning her room. One day in her hostel, the friends, unaware of this fact, try to surprise her by cleaning the room. She reacts vehemently to their surprise. This is one of the impacts of over-bonding parents who create an image of creepiness or endless interference on their account, toward the kids.

4.   Having No respect for the Kids: another category of poorly co-dependent parenthood is reflected through having no respect for the kids. This arises from a constant judgement of the kid being irresponsible, incompetent, unable and worthless, from the parent. Hence, the parent consistently makes remarks that emphasizes their lack of respect, honor and positivity towards the kid. This recurrent disapproval from the parent can mold the kid into a terribly depressed, clueless, dishonest and useless person with perpetual failures.

5. Comparing the kids with others: this is one of the worst aspects of poor parenthood, where the parents keep on comparing their kid's and expectation against the peer group of neighbor's, brother's, sister's, relative's kids grades, achievements and scores.

6. Biased relationship with kids: sometimes parents end up treating kids separately within the family. Exemplifying, in a family of kids- 1 boy and 1 girl, mother's undue affection towards the son, can instill a sense of abandonment for the girl child while a father's attachment towards the daughter can result in the son in the family feeling detached from the dad.

7. Control-freaks: yes, this category of co-dependent parents also exist. Parents who exert and execute their desires upon the dreams and ambitions of the kids figure into this category of control-freaks. They specify hard and fast rules that control the academic and personal life of their kids, without any relations, breaks or rewards for the same.

8. Recurrent punishments: another aspect of co-dependent parenthood is where the parents involve the kids in recurrent and regular punishments for their deeds. Control-freaks type of parents establishes hard rules, for which they make strict

punishments, regardless of the deed. This instils a sense of fear, hatred and discontent towards the parents.

9. Unsatisfied attitude: this arises from the perpetual comparisons and discontent from the parents towards their kids. Gradually the child ends up disbelieving in his or her abilities, skills, talents and dreams owing to the feeling of not making the parents ever happy. Lack of appreciation for good deeds, mature decisions and responsibilities bring about a constant depression and despair in the kid.

10. Perfectionists: some parents become too inflexible that they deny any fun or frolic to their kids. Their ideals of perfection remain the limits, restrictions and discontent for the kids. This inflexibility not only damages the parent-child relationship, but also brings about mentally unsatisfied kids.

Co-dependent Kids

Co-dependent kids are the kind of children who believe that their parents should be responsible for each of their deeds. Hence, they consult and counsel with their parents to achieve anything or take any a decision. This is due to their psychological belief of lacking confidence in the self about taking any decision by themselves. Co-dependent kids fear of the day that their parents will not be there, to guide them. Some of the main cause and effects of co-dependent behavior towards parents are:

1)   Worried Attitude: the first and foremost cause and effect of a co-dependent child is his worried attitude. The worried behavior is consistent regarding taking any a decision, doing anything or even forming an opinion about something.

2)   Perpetually Clueless: almost all co-dependent kids share this attitude as they feel clueless when they lack guidance from their parents. They do not know of an independent route or path unless guided by their parents beforehand.

3)   Empathies with parents too much: co-dependent kids empathies with their parents too much that their experiences are all lived by through their parent's shoes. Empathy involves relaxing one's own desires that the subject ends up feeling more than obliged to the parents.

4)   Call parents for everything: a co-dependent child ends up seeking his parents counsel under all circumstances, regardless of its importance. There is no independent identity, plan or resolutions and hence the child lacks any motive of the own, to achieve anything.

5)   Worried about crowd or loneliness: another primary defining aspect of a co-dependent child is his or her worry about facing the crowd or being lonely, in the absence of

parents. Co-dependent kids cannot are highly introverted sans their parents support.

6)   Love Addict: another important category of co-dependent children are the love-addicts, Casanovas or playboys. This kind of children become addicted to hunting for love due to the detachment they feel with their parents. Co-dependent children who miss their parents love, care and affection believes in being content through a relationship or constant dosage of intimacy shared with a person.

7)   Having parent's dream as own dream and none of the own: often, the kids who are overly co-dependent, end up believing in their own existence as something that is heavily obliged to making their parent's dreams come true.

8)   Self-sabotage: when a child ends up believing that parent's dreams, fantasies and desires are above their own, they end up sabotaging their own commitments, desires, fancies and whims to pave way for the parents dreams and ambitions coming true.

9)   No self-respect: a co-dependent kid has very low self-confidence, self-esteem and self-respect that he does not believe in his own potential of realizing his dreams, as there are none. Gradually such a kid turns into a terrible automaton without no individual aim, personal success or ambition.

Family as a Co-dependency Parameter

Co-dependent parenthood and co-dependent parent-child relationship in the longer run can induce a dysfunction in the entire family. Certain times the co-dependency manhandled in a marriage are a cause of dysfunction in the family. A co-dependence scenario of troubling parenthood gives rise to co-dependent kids who pave way for a dysfunction in the family, on a full scale.

Some of the harmful effects of dysfunction in a family due to co-dependence is through

1)   Lack of emotional contentment is one of the basic effects of a dysfunctional family as the kids and the parents both feel that the family is draining much of their positivity into it, rather than making themselves feel positive or content.

2)   Lack of Communication instils a huge gap in the family members as in the due course of time, each family member resorts to avoiding the company of the rest for one's own peace.

3)   Divorce: this is one of the direct effects of poorly handled marital co-dependencies. When co-dependency becomes irresolvable, parents can end up in suggesting divorce or separation, which can directly affect the physical, mental and emotional psyche of the kid.

4) De-valuing the suggestion of the family members: with the growing discomfort, individual members of the family ends up valuing the suggestions and remarks of other family members on a lesser and increasingly lesser honor.

5) Lack of Love: another important effect upon a family owing to inter-dependent co-dependent parameters is the experience of immense lack of love. This instils a feeling of needing to search for love outside the family, even becoming a love addict in the process.

6) Lack of Self-respect: another quite important aspect of co-dependency in a family is the lack of self-respect among individuals as well as lack of respect for each other. This induces a feeling of constantly minimizing the value of one's family as well as dismissing the same with worthlessness. This also instils in the family, a sense of lack of aims, ambitions and achievements.

7) Lack of Freedom individually, due to controlling, hard and punishing authoritarian patriarchy by the co-dependent parents/ kids;

Chapter 4 So, Are You Codependent?

Addiction to Food in Co-dependency

Food enablers are the co-dependent factors of increasing or adding to one's obesity or overeating disorders. Co-dependent partners that can add to one's eating disorders can be the parent, the kids, the partners or the friends. Due to the aforementioned harmful effects of co-dependency, some of the emotional imbalances of anxiety, restless, hypersensitivity, depression and stress can add to venting out the same through over-eating.

Spouses of the food-a-holics will try to please their partners by cooking exotic delicacies that render the subject and the partner to become obese on their own. Even though the co-dependent tries to limit the food intake of the partner and put down rules of healthy food diets, the love and other factors of co-dependent makes them the food enablers that lead to the obesity of both, in the due time. One's lack of communication and other misunderstanding inclusive of the intimacy issues can pull the reasons for venting out the aspects of anxiety through eating. Co-dependents should instead show the delight of delicacy through healthy diet.

Another theory of psychology dictates that co-dependency itself arises from a family dysfunction of overeating or obesity. When someone in a family has the habit of overeating, the children and other family members are also invited to the sumptuous dining, every time the food addict has a rush or pang, hence inducing the same overeating disorder in the rest of the family. This also teaches the family that overeating is a pleasant vent out or resolution for one's anxieties depression and stress.

Workaholics as part of co-dependency Parameter

Do you feel that the undue business tours and official appointments of our partner is leaving you lonely, unsatisfied, compromised and confined without any bliss in your relationship? Then your co-dependency is largely dependent on your partner's workaholic nature.

Workaholism is one of the biggest cause and effects of maintaining stability in a family, A workaholic patriarchal or simply, the head in a family enables the rest of the family to feel incomplete and discontent with the time spent with the workaholic. This induces a dissatisfactory co-dependence on account of the subject. They tend to adjust, compromise and fake affection to mask the absence and dissatisfaction with the concerned workaholic. Gradually, the rest of the family grown into a dysfunction of perspective that work is the only duty one should regard and respect. This instils a sense of detachment with morals, humanity, warmth and family values as each individual member of the family grows to regard their work of utmost importance.

Exemplifying, a highly workaholic businessperson father or mother can instill in their kids a sense of loneliness, detachment and ideology that is centered on the belief of delivering just productivity, money and profit as the morals of their life. The kid learns to regard his work more than his own family, and hence run to work even at his girl's deathbed.

Chapter 5 Getting Started in Recovery

While no two relationships are exactly the same, neither are codependent relationships. There is a great deal of diversity and variables within relationships, and at any given time, codependency can exist or not exist. This is why experts in the field of psychology have trouble identifying what exactly a codependent relationship is. What we do know is that people with certain personality types are prone to this type of relationship and that these habits are often learned early on, usually in childhood.

While it is possible for anybody to have healthy relationships, those who grew up with parents in healthy, well-adjusted relationships tend to have a leg up against those who were raised in a household constantly engrossed in emotional turmoil and disagreement. The idea of nature versus nurture says that the personality traits of a person are variable both by the genes of the person, but also the environment they grew up in. It would be hard to ignore the fact that a child would be affected by their environment, but also by genes from their parents.

While it may seem obvious that a child from a broken home would grow up and mimic the same habits, we must also consider the role that codependency between parent and child has on future relationships. Studies show that children who are coddled by their parents and who rely on the parents for everyday tasks will be attracted to a mate who will do the same for them.

If a parent consistently takes care of a child's every need, especially when doing things the child could easily do for themselves, they lack the confidence it takes to make it out on their own. This could be anything from cooking, cleaning, doing laundry, or even having the parents deal with conflicts between friends and classmates. When a parent plays too big of a role in their child's life, they actually teach them that they don't need to try, because someone will always be there to take care of them when times get tough. Unfortunately, as these children get older and begin looking for spouses, they look for someone they can depend on. While finding a mate you can rely on is a good trait, depending on them to do the things they can do themselves is selfish, and perpetuates the codependent relationship they had with the parent.

Another offshoot of this is with very strict parenting. Having a laundry list of rules to follow during childhood teaches discipline, but there is a fine line between learning life skills and becoming a prime candidate for a codependent relationship. Often times, if the rules are not followed, the parent can become angry or disappointed, and the child learns that they are doing well by the mood of the parents. The child can feel happy when they please their parents, and all self-worth is established through these means. The child's sole source of emotional well-being comes from the parents, and not from their own self-esteem. What they learn is that doing things right or wrong, in a very black and white way, is the basis of a good relationship. As they enter find spouses, they will carry out the same relationship. They become dependent on making their spouse happy, and if they don't their self-esteem diminishes. What perpetuates it even further is if their spouse depends on them to do simple tasks for them, making the relationship highly one-sided.

Certain personality traits are often seen in codependent relationships, and if you tend to relate to these traits, it may be time to take a closer look at your relationships. While it is not your destiny to be codependent, you may be more susceptible if you are a people pleaser. This type of person avoids conflict and will do whatever is necessary to avoid it. In childhood, these kids are often the teacher's favorite, never getting in trouble, as defying the rules would cause conflict and make their parents unhappy, the stem of their self-worth.

Further down the line, this person may fall victim to an emotionally of physically abusive relationship, as the burden of sticking up for themselves and ending a relationship would impose on their abuser. They would rather stay in the relationship than going through the conflict of ending it. Their self-esteem is so dependent on the wants and needs of their abuser, that leaving would cause inner turmoil as well, which is why so many people end up staying in these types of relationships.

People who are prone to depression or anxiety are also good candidates for codependency. Although the scientific community has not officially recognized codependency disorder as an official diagnosis, links are clear between mental disorders like anxiety and depression and codependency. This is likely because all three problems are usually caused by issues with self-esteem. When self-worth is defined by how you are perceived by others, it becomes difficult to cope with someone being unhappy with you. To remedy this, people often enter into codependent relationships in order to make them happy, or defying this lowers self-esteem, leading to anxiety and depression. Either way, it can be a very tough habit to break.

Codependency is also perpetual between generations. The environment you were raised in often dictates how you will raise your own children. The habits and parenting skills you were exposed to early on stick with you, and unless a valiant effort is made to teach your children a different way of life, you will likely end up parenting your kids the same way your parents raised you. In the case of a dysfunctional, codependent upbringing, this leaves little hope that your child will have a different life.

The good news is, once the habits you have developed can be recognized as dysfunctional or co-dependent, it becomes much easier to change those habits. You cannot stop what you don't recognize as a problem. Therefore, just by reading this book and recognizing that you may have some codependent habits, you can change that in yourself so that future generations will benefit from strong, healthy relationships with friends and loved ones.

Chapter 6 What Made You Codependent?

By now, you may recognize that you are in a codependent relationship. You may rely heavily on one friendship in particular, or pay extra attention to your spouse. It is natural to gravitate toward certain people, so don't overanalyze every relationship you are in. Still, it important to take stock of your relationships and begin to recognize if you are being used, or if you are using someone else. There are two sides to this equation, and it is important to establish healthy boundaries with friends and loved ones.

How do you know if you are being used? This one should be pretty simple to spot, but not always. Take inventory of your friends. Is there someone who consistently calls you for help with things? Looking after their kids? Getting yard work done? While you may be happy to help, is that person reciprocating the favors? If that person comes to rely on you to babysit, but never helps with your kids, or simply expects it from you, it may be time to set some boundaries. While that person may not be able to reciprocate in an appropriate manner, they should at least be grateful, and be cognizant of your time and energy.

In a spousal relationship, this may be harder to spot. In any relationship, roles are established early on. An over-eager spouse may want to take care of their loved ones every need, offering to cook, clean, wait on them hand and foot. While this may seem like a way to show affection, it can quickly turn into a codependent relationship. Unless the partner can reciprocate in some way, it may seem like the relationship is very one-sided. Over time, the over-eager spouse will become tired and a bit resentful that their partner is taking advantage of their good nature. However, by this time, they may feel like their self-esteem is reliant on how their spouse feels about them, likely a habit they developed earlier in life.

Being used can have many definitions. Someone may rely on you financially, or for help getting places if their car is broken. Your intentions are likely good, and just doing favors for someone doesn't mean you are codependent. You may be, however, if you start going out of your way, putting your own life on hold, to help someone else, especially when it is out of guilt. This is the ultimate definition of being used. Often times, if you are reliable and always there for someone, the moment you are not may make you feel guilty. This guilt could stem from your own feelings of inadequacy, or from the person you constantly help to make you feel guilty. Either way, the relationship has escalated to an unhealthy level, and it is time to set some boundaries. Yes, boundaries are discussed a lot, we will get to how to manage these relationships later on in the book.

This may be particularly difficult to pinpoint if a relationship has been this way most of your life. Of course, we are talking about a long-standing relationship between an adult child and their parents. It is important to stay in touch and take care of the people who raised you, but that relationship can get out of control as well. For example, let's say you suspect you may be in a codependent relationship with your own mother. In this case, your parents are divorced, and your mom lives on her own. She is constantly calling you to help mow the lawn and do daily tasks for her. You begin to forgo your own responsibilities to be at her beckoned call. One day, you decide to take a day trip with your own kids. Mom calls first thing in the morning and asks for help with something at her house. You explain that you are going out, but your mother makes you feel guilty, saying things like, " I only raised you", or "If it doesn't get done now, it will never get done", anything to make you feel guilty for having your own life. This type of relationship develops over time and is usually the result of codependency starting from early childhood. Your mother may not have had successful relationships in her past, specifically with her parents, and is bringing that to the relationship with you.

We often see this sort of relationship between mothers and their daughters in law. TV shows and movies have been dedicated to these relationships, in which the mother believes that nobody can take good care of her son, and anybody who tries is doomed to disappoint her. The mother is dependent on her son needing her for her own self-worth. Once she realizes that her son is grown and does not depend on her, she may lash out at his significant other, or the son, making both parties feel guilty for not spending more time.

How do you know if you are the user? Again, take stock of the relationships you are currently in. Is there one friend you always rely on to bail you out? Do you ever pay back the favor, or are you accustomed to them helping you? Another big one, do you feel upset when that person cannot help and do you give them an attitude, or act ungrateful when they can't step away?

In your personal relationship, do you expect your significant other to be with you all of the time? If they want to spend time with friends do you get jealous or upset? Do you make them feel guilty when they hang out with other people? These things may be difficult to face, and if they are, it is a good indicator that you are in a codependent relationship. If this sounds like you, it may mean that your self-esteem has been dictated by relationships like this in the past. It doesn't mean that this cannot be changed.

Perhaps one of the most difficult codependency relationships to deal with is one with addiction involved. If you are involved with someone with a drug addiction, gambling habit or something similar, it is likely that this person was not this way when you entered the relationship. Had you met them on the street in their current state, these facts would have been a major red flag for you to step away. Unfortunately, that person you are in love with was once a different person, and was not on drugs, or spending every night at gambling at the casino.

It is hard to come to terms with letting this relationship go because you see what was, and what potential is there in this person. Instead, you let the dysfunction continue, hoping that eventually, the person you knew and loved will come to their senses. This is exactly what happens with parents of drug addicts as well. Their sweet son or daughter is in there somewhere, and they are very susceptible to being manipulated by that person. That person will become dependent on their willingness to help, while their loved one becomes guilted into continuing to help them. Unfortunately, this just enables bad habits and the likelihood that they will snap out of it on their own is slim to none. If you make it easy for a drug user to continue abusing drugs, they don't have a good reason to stop.

Chapter 7 Healing Your Wounds — Freeing Your Self

In the last section, I examined the chart with circles and you should utilize this to assist you with deciding on whether you are being bona fide in your life or not, Remember, the inward circle speaks to your True Self. Nonetheless, your actual self is perpetually changing relying on the manner in which that you carry on with your life. In spite of the fact that the center you doesn't change, your mentalities change with time. The following circle is simply the depreciated and this is the place you at present are. You don't feel like you have that much worth and you sense that you don't have much decision in your life, however that is the place you are incorrect. On the off chance that you utilize the third circle and assess circumstances, you can gain from them and proceed onward from codependency so you turn out as the Ideal individual you might want to be.

The word perfect is abstract. One individual needs a certain something and another gets bliss from different things. To assist you with seeing what you get euphoria from, I might want you to plunk down and record the things you are appreciative for every day on the grounds that these will assist you with evaluating your situation from an increasingly positive point of view. Peruse your rundown of appreciation every prior day you endeavor to make yourself feel positive about what your identity is. At that point, take a gander at any circumstance that is giving you issues and work out the various situations which can prompt you turning into the perfect individual. How about we demonstrate to you a model,

You have a great deal of housework to do today. You feel overpowered. You additionally realize that there won't be sufficient cash to take care of the tabs this month.

This is your actual circumstance right now in time. What would you be able to do to transform it?

1) Get the housework done rapidly so you possess more energy for yourself.

2) Decide to set yourself an objective and keep it to the extent the housework is concerned.

3) Do the occupations that you realize will be taken note.

4) Look at your actual monetary circumstance so you are not stressed over something that truly isn't that awful.

5) Work out ways that you can spare a little to assist you with paying your bills.

6) Think about others much more terrible off who don't have a rooftop over their heads.

7) Think that you are so fortunate to have a home.

You have to work out your very own solutions to your own issues throughout everyday life, except you have to come to choices that help you to be not so much mutually dependent but rather more free. For instance, Nicole was in the very same circumstance as portrayed previously. She generally considered herself to be immaterial. Her first need was her better half who was a medication fiend. Everything went on his propensity. She had no cash left. What she didn't see was that it was conceivable to take care of the tabs just by removing something different of her spending. She was an awesome cook and figured out how to make heavenly dinners on a strict spending plan and set away enough cash so the bills could be paid without her better half realizing that she had held back. She really began to appreciate the cooking procedure and increased a great deal of fulfillment from the autonomy it gave her just as having the option to impart this to her better half. To the extent the housework was concerned, she gave herself a set time inside which to do the housework so she had time left over for herself. That was an irregularity. How she did this was to reveal to herself that what wasn't done by a set time would be left to one more day. She set objectives for critical things and did these, however really shocked herself at accomplishing more than she arranged.

Consistently you get difficulties. Consistently you get an opportunity to handle life in a superior manner that gives you more and there's nothing amiss with setting aside that effort for you. You have to develop your fellowships. You have to locate that perfect self that lies in the outside circle and when you do, you start to feel more grounded and progressively positive about yourself. While you are mutually dependent, you will in general put your very own needs on the back rack and that is never going to add to satisfaction. You will wind up detesting what you feel compelled to do with your life however it's just your codependence that powers you. On the off chance that you develop your very own confidence by permitting yourself a tad of delight – paying little heed to the conditions you are in – you can really give your adored one more since satisfaction checks. Glad individuals give more. Take a gander at the kinships you have with glad individuals and what you find is that you don't fear their visits. You don't feel awful about their inspiration. When you are upbeat, individuals will feel like that about you too.

No one but you can help yourself in this circumstance. Obviously, there are guides who are master in this field, yet this book is about YOU and what YOU can do individually to assist you with regaining the accompanying:

• Pride in yourself

• Happiness in your heart

• Gratitude for your life

• Love for yourself

What you may not understand is that codependency wrecks lives and it's not simply your life that is being destroyed. It is harmful and changes your general perspective on life and your connections and breeds so much lament, despondency and sharpness. By figuring out how to cherish yourself, you proceed onward and can carry on with a more joyful life and subsequently offer more to your loved ones than you ever could while you clutch the need to please others. Venture off the indirect that is wrecking your life and start to see past it.

I need you to return to part two and take a gander at the activity there where you need to choose the little things that you need to do in your life. These can be miniscule advances. They don't need to be colossal things. Possibly you deny yourself of things since you believe you don't merit them. Its rubbish, however it's what you accept. Right now is an ideal opportunity to break free from that servitude. Quit doing it to yourself and ensure that consistently, you do at any rate one thing that is your decision. It could be something as straightforward as:

• Treating myself to a peach

• Washing my hair and utilizing a conditioner

• Dressing in my pleasant garments

• Picking up the telephone and conversing with a dear companion

• Buying myself a lot of blossoms

• Eating a lot of grapes

• Trying out another eye cosmetic

• Practicing yoga

• Dancing before a stay in shape move video

You get one took shots at this life and it doesn't need to be drudgery. Quit causing yourself to do things that you despise any longer and allow yourself twenty minutes per day to accomplish something that you need to do. You need to rediscover the perfect you and you will never do that while you are mutually dependent. Your life doesn't rotate around the life of another person. It might interlace with the life of another person, however every individual is an island and that island takes into account fun here and there, just as obligation.

On the off chance that that is the manner by which you see yourself presently, it's an ideal opportunity to change your perspective. Obviously, you feel that you have to help your friends and family, yet the thing that matters is that a mutually dependent individual is eager to endure conduct that is in opposition to their prosperity. That is unfortunate, however it doesn't win you any pats on the back with the individual you make that penance for. Leave it speechless by figuring out how to cherish yourself.

Chapter 8 Welcome to the Real You

Be on guard for passing into our old practices. Codependency is dynamic; reusing can be as well. We can stall out, waste our time, at that point find we've gotten ourselves all the more profoundly settled in the refuse.

Regardless of whether our reusing knowledge keeps going six minutes or a half year, our natural response is normally one of refusal, disgrace, and self-disregard. That is not the exit plan.

That is the route in more profoundly.

We escape, or through, a reusing procedure by rehearsing acknowledgment, self-sympathy, and self-care. These demeanors and practices may not come as easily as disavowal, disgrace, and disregard. We've gone through years rehearsing disavowal, disgrace, and disregard. In any case, we can figure out how to rehearse more beneficial options, notwithstanding when it feels clumsy. A few proposals for doing that pursue.

Rehearsing Healthier Alternatives

The initial move toward traversing a reusing circumstance is distinguishing when we're in it. Here are some notice signs. 1

Feelings Shut Down. We may go numb and start solidifying or overlooking emotions.

We come back to the mentality that emotions are pointless, wrong, unjustified, or insignificant. We may reveal to ourselves very similar things about needs and needs.

Impulsive Behaviors Return. We may start habitually eating, caretaking, controlling, working, remaining caught up with, burning through cash, taking part in sexual practices, or whatever else we urgently do to abstain from inclination.

Unfortunate casualty Self-Image Returns. We may begin feeling, thinking, talking, and acting like an injured individual once more. We may start concentrating on others, or resort to accusing and scapegoating. A decent piece of information that I'm "in it" is the point at which I hear myself whimpering about how somebody is getting along either to me, or how terrible something is. My voice starts to grind on my nerves.

Self-esteem Drops. Our degree of confidence may drop. We may stall out in self-loathing or disgrace. We may turn out to be excessively disparaging of ourselves as well as other people.

Hairsplitting and sentiments of not being sufficient may return.

Self-Neglect Starts. Disregarding the little and huge demonstrations of self-care that are an ordinary piece of our recuperation routine may show we're near a reusing circumstance. Surrendering our day by day schedule is another sign.

The Crazies Return. All the old muck can return. This incorporates: return of tension and dread; feeling detached from individuals and our Higher Power; issues dozing (to an extreme or excessively little); personality hustling; feeling overpowered by perplexity (or just overpowered); trouble thinking plainly; feeling irate and angry; feeling regretful in light of the fact that we feel that way; feeling urgent, discouraged, denied, undeserving, and disliked. We may get into the "overs": overtired, exhausted, overcommitted, overextended, excessively delicate; or the "unders": came up short on, overlooked, underspent, starved, and sickly.

A proceeding with physical condition can be a notice sign that something is bothering at our psyches and feelings. We may start pulling back from and maintaining a strategic distance from individuals. An arrival to affliction or the "perseverance mode" is another notice sign. This would incorporate continuing the conviction that we can't appreciate life or have a ton of fun today, this week, or this month; life is something to be "traversed," and perhaps one week from now or one year from now we can be cheerful.

The Behaviors Return Too. When we're into a reusing circumstance, any or all the adapting practices may return.

Caught! Feeling caught, accepting we have no decisions, is an exceptionally speculate frame of mind.

Not That Again. It's conceivable to advance to the threat zone during reusing.

Side effects here incorporate incessant physical ailment, synthetic reliance, ceaseless despondency, or potential dreams about suicide.

After we've recognized an arrival to our old ways, the following stage is basic. We state,

"Uh oh! I'm doing it once more." This is called acknowledgment and trustworthiness. It's useful to come back to ideas like weakness and unmanageability as of now. In case we're working a Twelve Step program, this is a decent time to work Step One. This is classified "give up." Now comes the possibly troublesome part. We let ourselves know, it's alright, I did it once more. This is designated "self-sympathy."

Myths

Accepting any of the accompanying legends about reusing may make recuperation more troublesome than should be expected.

• I ought to be further along than I am.

• If I've been recouping for various years, I shouldn't have issues with this any longer.

• If I was working a decent program, I wouldn't do this.

• If I'm an expert in the recuperation, psychological wellness, or general helping field, I shouldn't have this issue.

• If my recuperation was genuine, I wouldn't do this.

• People wouldn't regard me on the off chance that they realized I thought, felt, or did this.

• Once changed, a conduct is gone until the end of time.

• I couldn't in any way, shape or form be doing this once more. I know better.

• Oh, no! I'm starting over from the beginning.

These are fantasies. On the off chance that we trust them, we have to attempt to change what we accept. It's alright to have issues. It's alright to reuse. Individuals who work great projects and have great recuperations reuse, regardless of whether they're experts. It's alright to do "it" once more, notwithstanding when we know better. We haven't gone right starting over from the beginning. Who knows? We may gain from it this time.

On the off chance that we demand accusing or feeling embarrassed, we can give ourselves a constrained time to do that. Five to fifteen minutes ought to be sufficient.

Dealing with Ourselves

After we've acknowledged ourselves and given ourselves an embrace, we pose ourselves two inquiries.

• "What do I have to do to deal with myself?"

• "What am I expected to learn?"

Regularly, oneself consideration ideas we have to practice are essential:

• acknowledgment,

• give up,

• reasonable assessment of what we can control,

• separation,

• expelling the person in question,

• managing emotions,

• paying attention to what we need and need,

• defining limits,

• settling on decisions and assuming liability for them,

• defining objectives,

• getting fair,

• giving up, and

• giving ourselves immense portions of affection and sustaining.

Intentionally concentrating on our recuperation program, conversing with sound individuals, employing ourselves with contemplations and positive musings, unwinding, and doing fun exercises help as well.

We have to recover our equalization.

Dealing with ourselves at work may require some unique contemplations than thinking about ourselves at home. Certain practices might be suitable at home yet could bring about loss of our activity. We might not have any desire to tell the manager how distraught we are at him. Self-care is self-obligation.

Codependency is a pointless cycle. Mutually dependent emotions lead to self-disregard, self-disregard prompts more mutually dependent sentiments and practices, prompting progressively self-disregard, and around we go. Recuperation is an all the more empowering cycle. Self-care prompts better sentiments, more beneficial emotions lead to progressively self-care, and around that track we travel.

I don't know unequivocally what you have to do to deal with yourself. In any case, I realize you can make sense of it.

Something else I don't know is the thing that exercise you're learning. It's everything I can do to get familiar with my own. I can't reveal to you how to understand the specific encounters throughout your life, yet I can disclose to you this: among you and your Higher Power, you will make sense of that as well.

Try not to stress. In the event that you don't comprehend, or in the event that you aren't prepared to become familiar with your exercise today, that is alright. Exercises don't leave. They continue introducing themselves until we learn them. What's more, we'll do that when we're prepared and all is good and well.

Tips

In spite of the fact that I don't have a recipe for self-care and learning life's exercises, I've gathered a few hints that may help during reusing.

• If it feels insane, it likely is. Regularly when we keep running into an insane framework, our first response is still to think about what's up with us. We can confide in certain individuals, yet we can't confide in everybody. We can confide in ourselves.

• If we're ensuring ourselves, something might undermine us. Possibly a trigger is helping us to remember the past times or an old message is attacking us. Here and there, somebody in our present is undermining us, and we're attempting to imagine they're most certainly not. In case we're ensuring ourselves, it gets who or what is frightening us, and what we're shielding ourselves from.

• When one strategy for critical thinking falls flat, attempt another. Once in a while, we stall out.

We experience an issue, choose to explain it a specific way, come up short, at that point more than once, once in a while for a considerable length of time, attempt to take care of that issue similarly, despite the fact that that way doesn't work. Regroup and take a stab at something different.

• Self-will doesn't work any preferred during recuperation over it did previously. Giving up works. In some cases in reusing, we're experiencing the way toward denying an issue that is crawling into our mindfulness. We're attempting to stay away from it or defeat it by applying more prominent measures of self-will. At the point when self-will comes up short, attempt give up.

• Feelings of blame, pity, and commitment are to the mutually dependent as the primary beverage is to the heavy drinker. Watch out for what occurs straightaway.

• Feeling pitiful and baffled since we can't control a person or thing isn't equivalent to controlling.

• Trying to recover our misfortunes for the most part doesn't work. "On the off chance that I think back and gaze at my misfortunes excessively long, they gain on me," says one man. "I've figured out how to take them and run."

• We can't at the same time set a limit and deal with the other individual's feelings.

• Today isn't yesterday. Things change.

• We don't need to accomplish more today than we can sensibly do. In case we're worn out, rest. In the event that we have to play, play. The work will complete.

Chapter 9 Building Self-Esteem and Self-Love

People usually consider themselves as caring people. They express the care through actions. There is, however, a little known and darker side to this act of caring for other people and which is neither talked about enough nor well fathomed.

One behavior associated with codependency is caretaking – which is not ideal – and should be replaced by caregiving. Codependency causes you to have unhealthy relationships, and caretaking is one of those qualities that should not be exercised.

Differences between Caregiving and Caretaking

There are vital differences between caregiving and caretaking. In a healthy relationship, the happier and healthier you both are, the more you do caregiving rather than caretaking. Caretaking is a dysfunctional behavior that can still be changed. It should be lessened, or better yet, eliminated if possible. Your objective is to do as much caregiving and as less caretaking as you can – in order to experience more contentment, peace and happiness in your relationships.

Caregiving

When someone needs care and assistance, whether caused by a chemical dependency, chronic medical state, or being cured from any illness, the one who provides the nurturing is called the caregiver. The caregiver is possibly a friend, family member, or health professional. This person gives support and comfort to another when necessary. The assistance is provided with kindness and compassion, emerging from a place filled with love and without any expectations of receiving something as payment. Caregivers can rely on and acknowledge the patient's position on his or her chosen path and will not meddle nor try to change it.

Caretaking

A caretaker also extends a helping hand when needed. He can be a friend, family member, or professional. This person gives what he or she thinks as comfort and support, and usually waits for something in return -- he "gives to get". A caretaker may attempt to modify the outcome and not allow the patient's path take its natural course. Through a caretaker's eyes, what he or she does is out of love; however, there is possibly a subconscious or underlying motive of fear.

Here are other ways on how you can distinguish caregiving from caretaking:

Caretaking

- Worry
- Crosses boundaries
- Think they understand what's best for other people

- Immediately rush into action when a problem comes up
- Consider self-care as a selfish act, and therefore avoids it
- Usually attracts needy people
- Focuses on the problem
- Uses "you" a lot

Caregiving

- Solve problems and take action
- Respects boundaries
- Only know what's good for themselves
- Wait to be asked for help before taking action
- Practice self-care to take care of others
- Usually attracts healthy people
- Focuses on the solution
- Uses "I" more

You cross the line between caregiving and caretaking when your personal energy is channeled to others who are perfectly able of taking care of themselves. This is usually triggered by caring too much, or the choice of doing more than you should as caring, when in fact, it is already caretaking.

What makes caretaking so hard to detect by the untrained eye to spot is about the actions of the person being camouflaged under the idea of caring. More often than not, the person who's also a caretaker is unaware of what they are doing simply because it feels a lot like love and intimacy although it's actually not.

Of course, you always want to have a smooth flowing relationship. No one wants to be with someone who's unhappy all the time. You care and provide all the attention that you can shower to your partner. But how do you know if it's no longer "caring", but instead being "codependent"?

Problems start to arise when helping starts to feel hurting; you feel fear, and this is where your relationship is based on. Clearly, this isn't good, as this ends up not being healthy for everyone involved. Simply put, caretaking starts from insecurity. It's a codependency hallmark wherein you are in a need to be in control. Caregiving, on the other hand, is an illustration of love and kindness.

For a caretaker, it can be quite a revelation to realize that it's better to be liked and appreciated for who you are, instead of being liked and appreciated just because you gave someone what he or she needed at that time. Being with someone doesn't have to come with reasons or conditions.

Chapter 10 Finding Pleasure

Identifying a codependent relationship is tricky. It is often disguised in any individual's willingness to adapt to other people's needs.

People in general consciously or unconsciously assign all the people in their lives a role to assume. They then deal with these people based on what they think these people want from them. In essence, it's like presenting a puppet show of your life. You may not realize it, but you are orchestrating the whole show based on what you conceptualize in your head.

There are people who are somewhat oblivious of the "roles" they assume, some seem to be detached, and others run along the lines of being codependent. In order to put an end to or overcome a codependent relationship, you need to recognize a person who "suffers" from codependency.

You will find in the succeeding paragraphs some of the most common codependent "roles." Do not be surprised if you recognized yourself in more than one. In addition, you will find some strategies on how you can change the script so nobody becomes the codependent party.

1. Martyr

For martyrs, suffering is virtuous. They are happy when they were able to put the needs of their loved ones ahead of their own. They are the ones who would be the first one to take on an extra project and always the last person to leave the office. They would pick up the tab voluntarily even if they are broke. Recognize the signs? It might have been the concept that your parents and your religious belief has instilled in you.

The Issue: You might not have realized it yet, but when sacrifice is your norm when it comes to relationships with loved ones, friends, and colleagues, you tend to neglect your own needs to be loved and cared for. While these are the things that you are hoping to get by giving more than you can give, chances are your efforts can backfire. When you don't get what you want from the relationship, you'll begin to resent these very same people to whom you've extended your help.

How to Overcome: Begin to care for yourself

It is important that you understand the difference between self-care and selfishness. You have to realize that you are not being selfish if you opt to leave the office on time or if you want to go out with friends once in a while. Also, it isn't rude if you ask to split the bill if you can't afford to shoulder everything. You have to begin to care for yourself because no one else will. Ernest Hemingway, an American author and journalist, once said, "My health is the main capital I have and I want to administer it intelligently." If we don't have our health, we have nothing left to give. It's similar to the idea of how to respond to an emergency in a plane crash: put on your oxygen mask first before helping others or else you are no help to either of you.

2. Savior

A savior takes pride in being the one to solve all conflicts. He is the one who's always there to lend money when a friend needs it, even if he is equally broke.

The Issue: There is no denying that everyone does need help sometimes and it is not bad to help. However, if you feel it is your personal mission to be the one to give comfort to others, even to the point of creating discomfort on your part, it is not healthy. You are telling the people you've helped that they are hopeless without you. You teach them to become overly dependent on you. As a result, you've created a relational dynamic that will continuously suck energy, time and resources out of you. People can learn to take advantage of this. They can even manipulate you to get what they want. When people get used to you being their savior, they quickly react when you don't perform that role in their life.

How to Overcome: Empower

It is always a good thing to help; it's a win-win situation because you feel good when you are able to be of help. However, you have to examine your real purpose for helping other people. It is also important to analyze if it is also doing them good. Being there for them is one thing but preventing them from being self-reliant is another. There are people whom you have helped once who come in for another and then another until they are totally dependent on you that they do nothing to improve their own situation. It's not rude to occasionally say "no." When you save people from their problems, you may actually be robbing them of a lesson that they need to learn for themselves. If you feel that helping other people is the only time that you are needed and loved, then you are not in a healthy relationship at all.

3. Adviser

Are you an adviser? You probably have an ability to look into someone else's problems and offer solutions and advice. The adviser is not too good a listener, though.

The Issue: People come to you because you give good advice. You feel happy because they constantly come to you to hear what you have to say. You assume that they lack self-esteem to even solve their own problems. In reality, though, advisers are the ones who are really insecure and they feel needed when people come to them. They are the ones who lack self-esteem. They want to feel in charge and in control and the only way they can do that is to tell someone what they have to do.

How to Overcome: Set boundaries

If someone comes to you and pours their heart out, try to listen to them for a change. Just by listening, you are able to help your friend or your loved one. You don't have to tell them what to do. Let them make the decision themselves. Let them see for themselves the perfect solution to their problems. You can give them your two cents' worth but only after you have listened to them, and do not tell them what to do. Give them options and then let them decide. Do not tell them outright that they have to do this or that. Respect their own judgment; be a friend and just listen. Ultimately, people need to come to their own conclusions about their problems.

4. People Pleaser

The people pleaser is the one who always volunteers to organize something for the community. They are the ones who volunteer to fix everything. They bask in the glory of being "appreciated" for their hard work in initiating gatherings, parties, and fund drives.

The Issue: It is not really a problem if you are the go-to person when it comes to social gatherings, but it becomes a problem when you begin to feel that doing so becomes a chore yet you cannot say "no" because you don't want them to stop liking you. People-pleasing is passive manipulation. You do things for other people because you can get something from them.

How to Overcome: Learn to Say No

It is not your loss if you say "no." The next time the office needs a volunteer, think twice before stepping up to do the task. Analyze if people are indeed going to dislike you if you didn't volunteer. Are you up for another task? Don't you have other important things to do at home? Learn to say "no" not because you don't want to do it but because there are other more important things that you need to do. There is always a time for everything. Besides, the world won't fall apart if you say "no." You can be replaced. People are capable of finding other people to help.

5. The Person who Says "Yes" All the Time

Have you ever been in a situation when you had to say "yes" when you really wanted to say "no?" Did you resent your action? A person who says "yes" all the time is one who keeps his discomfort to himself.

You can't tell your friends what you really feel for fear of offending them. You can tell your partner that you are upset because you didn't want to start a fight.

The Issue: A healthy relationship is one in which both parties or a group of friends are in total honesty with each other. If you avoid conflicts so you just say "yes" when you meant to say "no," there is a disconnect somewhere in the honesty department there.

In the office, there is something that you are uncomfortable with but you are too afraid to tell your boss for fear that you might lose your job. With your partner, you are afraid to trigger an argument because you fear that they might leave you. So, you hide the feelings inside. When this happens, you might end up resenting them and eventually ruin your relationships.

How to Overcome: Be Honest

If you don't speak up, you will not resolve anything. Your partner might not be aware that there is a problem already until it blows up in your faces. It takes courage to tell the truth but it is liberating. You can tell the truth without hurting someone else's feelings. Talking about a problem doesn't always equate to creating conflicts; this is just the healthier way of bringing up unresolved issues to find solutions.

Did you identify yourself in any of these? You were able to hurdle the first step to making changes in your life: awareness of the "problem." Acceptance that there is a problem is critical in making improvements.

Reclaiming Yourself from Codependency

People become codependent longer than they should because they are scared of being alone or feel accountable for their partner's happiness. They may say their desire to break free – but end up staying instead. Others may go away but end up committing the similar self-damaging mistakes once they get in a new relationship. The adrenaline rush felt when they experience passionate feelings toward someone can be captivating. For a lot of people, the rationale behind extreme emotional reliance on a partner is codependency – a tendency to put other's needs before their own.

No matter how hopeless it may appear, codependent people can still break free from their emotional struggles. Regardless of how low they may have felt during their worst moments, they can still recover from this condition.

Raising Your Self-Esteem

Self-esteem is an assessment of someone's worth, or how an individual judge himself. It's also defined as a person's competency in coping with life's basic challenges, and deserving of happiness. Self-esteem one of codependency's main symptoms, and it has to be addressed as soon as possible.

Codependents often have sensitive self-esteem combined with the fear of abandonment or rejection. The "esteem" they have is based on how others see them and perceive their character. They live by solving problems of other people, and this boosts their morale in a distorted way. If something goes awry, they take the blame and bear the guilt. They fill up their schedule to focus on one person – they have this feeling of being needed, and this feeling overcomes everything else.

Codependents usually come from dysfunctional, troubled, or repressed families. They deny it, though, hence the failure of solving their personal issues brought by them being codependents.

They take the blame for almost everything yet also blames others for everything. They reject compliments but are saddened when they don't get complimented. They are scared of being rejected yet reject themselves. They don't think they will be loved or liked, so they tend to show others they are lovable enough to be accepted by other people.

How should you reclaim your self-esteem?

- Challenge any self-defeating thoughts or beliefs about self-worth. You don't have to confirm anything to anyone about yourself.

- See yourself in a loving relationship that fulfills your desires and meets your needs. If your present relationship is damaging, look at ways on how you self-sabotage and observe your own behaviors.

- Tell yourself everyday that it's healthy to receive help from others, and it's an indication of strength rather than weakness. Friendships, counseling, and other online resources can be ultimately helpful to guide you in looking for a happy relationship.

- Become aware of any negative judgments you have about yourself. Don't be harsh; you have to be kind and compassionate on yourself.

- Don't be afraid of rejection; go ahead and get involved in intimate and loving relationships. Concede and let go of your shield, and allow others in your life.

Have you considered that you're just hooked on the pain brought by love? If yes, then remind yourself that you risk your chances of having happy and healthy relationships where your needs can be fulfilled. Are you afraid of being alone? Are you scared of taking a risk? By doing so, you prevent yourself from seeking the happiness and love you deserve.

Focus on your healing and your personal growth – by doing so, you'll begin to transform your life and attract others who are in the same emotional level as you.

Overcoming Guilt and Resentment

Sometimes, guilt is good. Guilt can make people empathize, take the right course of action and to make themselves better individuals. After guilt, forgiveness of oneself should always follow as it's an essential key to life and relationships. For many, however, self-acceptance still remains hard to get hold of due to unhealthy guilt, and this guilt can stay with a person for years, decades, or even for a lifetime.

Guilt is a possible persistent source of pain. You keep on reminding yourself to condemn yourself and to be guilty, and it ends up destroying you and meddling with your goals. Guilt brings anger and resentment, not only to yourself but to people around you.

Why should negative feelings such as guilt, resentment and anger be avoided? One, they absorb your energy. Two, they bring illness and depression. Three, they prevent you from having happiness, success and fulfilled relationships. They hinder you from moving on and stop you from moving forward.

Codependents usually have guilt within them. It's common for them to accept the blame and feel responsible for another's wrongdoings because of their lack of self-esteem. Guilt, however, should be differentiated with shame; shame is when you feel inadequate and inferior, and tends to underestimate yourself and your relationships.

How do you overcome these feelings of shame, guilt and resentment? Ask these questions to yourself, and follow the steps.

- Take responsibility if you've been rationalizing your actions. Tell yourself, "Yes, I did it." Look back and remember what happened. Think about how you felt, and think about other people involved in the process. Consider what were your needs during those times, and if they were met. If those needs weren't met, then why weren't they? What were your motives in doing so? Was there any catalyst for such behavior? Is this catalyst connected to a person or an event in your past? You can write them all down, with a dialogue that includes your feelings.

- While growing up, how were your feelings and mistakes handled? Were you judged for them? Punished? Forgiven? Were people hard on you because of those mistakes? Were you somehow made to feel ashamed?

- How do you judge yourself? Are they really based on your personal faith and principles, or are they based on someone else's approval? Do you still need someone else's support before you go for something that you like? Don't aim to live up on another person's expectations – there are instances on which you'll never get their approval, and in doing so, you might end up sacrificing your own happiness and wants.

- Are your current actions matched with your true values? If not, think of your thoughts, emotions and beliefs that made you do your actions. What may have led you to abandon your values? In violating your values, you end up hurting yourself, which is more painful than hurting someone else.

- How did these conflicts affect you and other people? Take note of those people that you've hurt, and remember that you've hurt yourself as well. Reflect on how you can make amends and ask forgiveness from these people – how can you make things better? Can you still do something to ease the pain?

- If someone did you wrong, you'd possibly forgive them easily. Why then would you treat yourself differently? Do you think it benefits you to punish yourself continually?

- There's nothing wrong with making mistakes as long as you learn from them. Remorse is acceptable – even healthy – and it leads to creating corrective action. You'll learn how to act differently. Write yourself a letter filled with appreciation, understanding and forgiveness. Repeat these words to yourself: I forgive myself. I'm innocent. I love myself.

- Surround yourself with people who won't judge you for your past. Share to them what you did. Avoid secrecy to avoid further prolonging guilt and shame.

What is a healthy and humble attitude? You believe you're at fault but you still forgive yourself. Others were wrong, yet you forgive them. You regret the things that happened in the past yet you understand it was just a part of being human, and you ended up learning from your mistakes and you gain experience.

Yes, that is a healthy attitude.

Separating Responsibilities

Another vital task that codependents have to understand is how to separate responsibilities for themselves and for others. They react on other people's concerns. As these problems become more intense, codependents' reactions are more intense as well. They tend to be more involved in the process, hence keeping them in a chaotic state, as well as the people around them. Their energies are focused on other people and their problems which makes them less attentive to their own lives.

In rescuing, codependents aim to take care of people who can perfectly live their own lives. They dwell on problems they don't have control over, and can be upset when things go wrong. What they don't know is that rescuing these people from their responsibilities doesn't help them grow but instead makes them evade the outcome of their actions more. Love makes codependents undertake in manipulative behavior. Their intentions are to help, and they end up being people who force things to happen using too much effort and energy.

Codependents fail to realize that other people don't need controlling, and these people would usually have no interest in obtaining the outcome the Codependent is aiming for. Codependents must understand as well that people will simply do what they wish to do regardless if they're wrong or right, or if they're hurting themselves.

Codependents who do another person's task doesn't help the person be better by rescuing them -- they instead actually teach them to be more dependent, and will lead to them taking advantage of the Codependent. In return, the codependent becomes resentful, overburdened, and ultimately vengeful and upset simply because they do things they don't wish to do.

Chapter 11 Letting Go and Non-attachment

As people grow up, they learn to become more independent. Life events such as college, marriage, and having a family are trademark examples of a person becoming independent. However, codependent people struggle to reach the average person's independence. This can be problematic for a number of reasons because independence has major benefits. One benefit is independence can boost a person's confidence. When a person is learning to become more independent, this means that they are learning to rely on themselves. This leads to the person needing to become more sure and self-reliant in their decision making. This, in turn, leads to the person building their confidence.

Another reason why confidence is important is that it can lead to a person to become less reliant on other people. The most obvious explanation for why this is true is when a person becomes more independent, they do not need to rely on other people as much as they used to be. As a result, the person is able to learn that it is okay to be on their own and they are also more likely to appreciate another person's help when it does happen, especially when help is needed.

Independence is also a way to alleviate a person's stress levels. Once a person no longer needs to constantly rely on other people, they are less likely to be dissatisfied or stressed out when they are making plans. They only need to rely on themselves.

One other way independence can be beneficial is because of self-value is improved. When a person becomes more independent, they are able to trust their instincts and themselves in general. Trusting one's self shows that they value themselves and their ability to make decisions. People also tend to feel accomplished when they work through something on their own.

For the people who struggle with independence, there are ways to improve reliance on one's self. It can be uncomfortable and overwhelming to take the necessary steps to independence, but the end result is worth the hard times in the beginning.

The first way to improve someone's independence is to take the time to learn more about one's self. People can feel unsure of who they are. This is especially true for codependent people because their identity is usually attached to whoever they have become dependent on. A person might find that they tend to say yes or no to things that they do not necessarily want to do because they are so focused on appeasing other people.

A great way to learn more about one's self is to start journaling. The main benefits of doing this are that the person will begin to understand how they are feeling, why they make certain behavioral decisions, and why they act in certain ways. This will lead to independence because the person will begin feeling more confident in knowing who they are and understanding how their thought patterns work. Reflecting on how one feels and thinks about certain situations also lead to a new level of trust the person has in themselves and their instincts. The person will also likely learn more about what they want out of life that meets their own needs rather than someone else's needs. The end result of understanding one's self is the person will also be able to reason which areas of their life should take on more independence and when the independence should begin setting in.

Another way to become more independent is to stop asking other people for permission. While there are instances where a second opinion is welcome, it is important that people learn to think for themselves and not relying on other people to do the decision making. Once a person learns to stop asking other people for permission, then they can gain independence. This is because when a person stops relying on other people to make plans, they are, in turn, learning to trust that their own mind and emotions can make the best decision for a given situation.

If a person is too dependent on getting other people's opinions or permission, then they have become overly dependent on the other person's ideas. This will not help a person gain independence; it actually hurts their chances of reaching independence. When people ask for someone else's opinion or permission, they probably already have the same idea in their own head. Their goal is to gain the approval of the other person. This means that the next time a person is looking to ask for someone's permission or approval, they should look at their own answer first and go along with their instincts. When a person is able to be more aware of their instincts then their thoughts and emotions seem more reliable as well. There becomes no need to ask for permission, which means their independence is strengthened.

The next way to become more independent is if the codependent person learns how to be more assertive with other people. When a person becomes confident that someone will agree with them or not tell them "no," then they might start to become dependent on that individual. Codependent people are notorious for being agreeable with other people in order to avoid being abandoned or rejected. Once the codependent person is able to stop themselves from always giving in to what other people want, a newfound independence will take its place.

One's ability to learn how to be more assertive will actually allow them to know when to tell a person "no" and when it makes sense for them to say "yes." In turn, the codependent person can see when it is important for them to put themselves first.

Learning how to puts one's own needs before other people, when necessary, can lead to not only independence but self-value as well. Codependent people can become so dependent on helping other people and putting their needs ahead of one's own needs. This can lead to the codependent forgetting about themselves and what they actually want to be doing.

It is important to be assertive in relationships and with other matters of life. For example, if a codependent person finds that a fellow employee is asking them to take care of work that is not the codependent person's responsibility, this may be because the fellow employee knows the codependent person says "yes" often. This can lead to unnecessary stress for the codependent person.

The codependent person should start saying "no" more often so that they can focus more on their own needs. They should also remember that the people who truly care for the codependent person will accept when they say "no" and want the codependent person to take the time to look after themselves.

Setting aside time for alone time and alone dates can also lead to independence. The codependent can go about doing this by thinking about doing certain things that they normally do with others. It could be responsibilities such as grocery shopping or running errands, but the alone dates could also be going to a coffee shop and catching up on some reading over a cup of coffee or going to a movie.

The act of fitting in some alone time not only allows the person to increase their independence and feeling comfortable with one's own company, but alone dates can improve a person's confidence and self-esteem.

When codependent people set aside time once a month to take advantage of alone dates, then they can build up their sense of self-worth. This also means that the codependent person no longer needs to wait for other people to be available to do something; they only need to depend on themselves to be ready.

Alone dates can also be viewed as a form of self-love because the codependent person is showing themselves that they are comfortable being alone and themselves in general. The act of being alone is actually great when to let go of the negative and shameful thoughts that often arise when a codependent person finds themselves alone.

One final way to build a codependent person's independence is to provide emotional support for one's self rather than seeking support from someone else. It is not only true for codependent people but others as well, to seek help from other people when one is feeling down or overwhelmed. The mind believes that other people can provide them with the comfort and advice that will lift their spirits. There is nothing wrong or abnormal about turning to other people for support. However, when a person becomes too dependent on receiving support from other people rather than turning to one's self for support, then this will only fuel their codependent tendencies.

It is extremely important to learn how to gain support from one's self because once a person is capable of getting emotional support from themselves then they will learn how to take control of their emotions and the course of their life. A person's ability to comfort themselves rather than relying on other people to do so is actually how a person can achieve emotional support from one's self.

The emotional support a person gains from themselves can prove to them that they are not only capable of physically taking control of their life, but mentally they can as well. This is especially rewarding for codependent people because their mind is the largest obstacle standing in their way of trusting in their self.

Once a person takes the necessary steps towards gaining independence, then they too can reap the benefits that independence can bring them. It will take time and effort to work through the mental barriers preventing codependent people from maintaining independence. Yet, it is important to push through the discomfort and fear in order to trust in one's self.

- Knowing they are unique and comfortable in their skin.

- Holding firm boundaries to maintain their self-esteem and self-worth.

If you are codependent, you may ask other people their opinion of something that only you can answer about yourself. You might beat yourself up and disregard compliments if others direct them toward you. Codependents lack self-esteem, which means they often doubt themselves and their ability to grow. They don't feel worthy enough to try new things, and they lack boundary control. Having low self-esteem can affect all aspects of one's life, which can lead to a downward spiral of continuous negative habits. However, you can learn and develop self-esteem over time and with effort, you can transform it into self-worth and confidence.

One of the first steps to achieving this goal in building self-esteem is to detach yourself from codependency. If you are codependent, you first need to realise that you cannot solve everyone's problems. If you are involved with a codependent, then creating healthy boundaries and learning the signs can help you evaluate your deterring strategies.

Disengage with Love and Kindness

When you hear the word detach, you might think of it as disappearing, pushing away, or withdrawing. Staying away from codependency doesn't mean you need to do any of these;

it means to let go of the characteristics of codependency. These include letting go of control, anxiety and excessive worries, blame, or feeling ashamed and guilty for everything. Think of detachment from codependency as distancing yourself from what makes you prone to codependent traits but still keeping your real sense of self. To do this, give yourself some boundaries. Every time you catch yourself trying to control people or situations, stop and think about how you can do things differently. Every time you obsess and avoid things, fight against these enforced thoughts and don't avoid or obsess. While all this seems easier said than done, it will take mindfulness and practice to get it right. Some examples of the disengaging processes are:

Emotionally

- Only do things according to what you can control; the rest isn't worth stressing about.

- Avoid making snap decisions regarding important life events. For example, instead of making a spontaneous decision, think about it for a few hours.

- Instead of controlling everything, give the control to someone else and ignore the itch to jump in.

- Allow others to make choices for themselves.

- The only problems that you can control are your own, give advice but don't take other's issues into your own hands.

- Question your expectations of yourself. Are they unrealistic and far-fetched?

   Physically

- Walk away to breathe after a disagreement or rising conflict.

- Choose against visiting a toxic person in your life.

- Do not get yourself into compromising situations.

Codependency takes years of brain wiring and restructure, as habits form and take residence in your memories, promoting unstable patterns throughout your life. Detaching yourself from codependency will take courage, effort, and resilience. Remember to congratulate yourself after every accomplishment; this will help your brain reconnect the neurons that your past and experiences have damaged. While you work on viewing codependency as a toxic friend that is not a part of you, building self-esteem and confidence can help in ridding yourself of codependent habits for good.

Building Self-Esteem

It's not just codependency that can stem from a traumatic childhood; low self-esteem also resembles trauma. Any form of neglect or lack of attention while in the early development years can trigger low self-esteem. Starting at an early age, we learn from behaviors, methods, and parental guidance. Sometimes, families can be dysfunctional, which alters the young mind to view the world as a scarier place than it is, which makes no room for imperfections. From having a low view and reflection of oneself, people can miss out on opportunities they don't feel confident enough to accomplish. This results in feeling powerless to change things as they also don't feel confident enough to handle such a significant change. Here are some things you can do to boost your self-esteem.

Challenge the Inner Critic

Most of the time, low self-esteem is believing in your negative thoughts. These negative thoughts are the voice behind the cruel inner critic who defeats you for everything you do and makes you doubt yourself in your quest for success. Despite what your internal critic says to you, you must think about everything you have overcome. Think about your achievements, the problems you have solved (even if they weren't yours) the positive relationships you have created, and quiet the bully by reminding yourself that you have strengths too. When your brain says, 'you can't do that,' challenge it by saying 'I will try.'

Take Care of Yourself

Taking care of your physical wellbeing can also promote mental and spiritual wellbeing. Part of taking care of your physical self is paying close attention to your hygiene and your appearance. When you look good, you feel good. However, do not go overboard in needing to have every blemish covered up;

instead, be okay with the things that make you stand out. Make sure your clothes are clean and smell nice. Eat healthy food that boosts your immunity and overall mood. Take care of the stress that seems to weigh you down. Keep an exercise schedule and continue to increase serotonin levels through healthy workouts. Do things you enjoy or that you are good at.

If you don't know what you are good at doing, make a list of all your strengths and achievements. Within that list, you will see the hidden talents you might have that you didn't know about. For example, your list could look like this:

- Got Λ's in Maths and English.

- Won a sporting award at school.

- Got promoted at my job.

- Helped a friend move to a new house.

- Painted a masterpiece.

-

Within the list of achievements, you can see that you are good at Maths and English, you excelled at painting, and you were helpful towards your companions. When you choose what to do next, try painting another picture, creating a blog, or building a business plan. Are you more creative, or are you more of a critical thinker? Can you revise your finances or help a friend budget? Do things you exceed at and your self-esteem will increase because you feel good about these things.

Try New Things

Trying new things can be a scary experience for some people because they are afraid of failure. Most codependents help others work on new things and observe on the sidelines because that's how they define their self-esteem. However, instead of watching someone do something new, join in with them. Have you ever gone on a road trip just for fun with no destination? Have you ever walked up to a stranger and started a conversation? Think of something you're good at, but also something you fear, and dip your toes in. When you accomplish something new, your self-esteem will rise, especially when you reward yourself after every attempt, even if you fail.

Avoid Toxicity

As much as a codependent likes to avoid things, they don't avoid toxicity. To reverse this behavior, pay attention to the underlying problems that you have avoided. Replace natural avoidance patterns with avoiding toxic people and toxic habits instead. This method is a great technique to boost self-esteem and confidence levels. Another way you can avoid toxic people is to create solid boundaries and learn to put your foot down. Codependent personalities are prone to having people take advantage of them, so if a codependent can learn to identify toxicity and walk away, it can help in breaking the abusive cycle. As much as people can be toxic, situations can also be toxic. A toxic situation can be where you don't feel safe, someone is bullying you, or there is always a crisis happening. In these circumstances, the best thing to do is practice your mindfulness strategies, then plan your escape route. Once you get yourself out of the dramatic situation, you can work on some relaxation methods like deep breathing, taking a bath, and talking to a close friend. When your mind is fresh and bright, start by avoiding the toxic triggers that lead you into the situation, to begin with. Other aspects that can gain self-love, self-esteem, and confidence are learning how to respect yourself and acknowledge your self-worth.

Acknowledging Self-Worth

Self-esteem and self-worth are very similar in the fact that they both reflect how we feel about ourselves. However, self-worth is knowing that you have the power and control to make all of what you think (or don't think) about yourself happen. For example, if you lack self-esteem, it means that you don't feel competent enough to see yourself as a unique and reliable individual. If you lack self-worth, it means that even if you had the drive to accomplish all your goals and dreams, you don't feel like you deserve to have them. Self-esteem can be defined and increased by what you do and how you carry yourself and your behaviours. Whereas, self-worth is determined by what you believe can be done and accomplished by what you feel you deserve. In short, self-worth is more about who you are not defined by what you do.

Much of building self-worth is by developing your self-esteem; however, to acknowledge your self-worth is to believe that you deserve respect and validation. Self-worth is the fundamental point of self-acceptance. So, gaining some insight into developing more self-worth, recognise when those thoughts of comparison creep through. When your mind says 'you will never be a superstar' challenge it with, 'I already am.' You don't have to believe this thought straight away; defeat your inner critic one idea at a time. Another way to build self-worth is knowing when to have compassion for yourself and when to push yourself forward. When we do too much of one thing, we are striving for perfection. When we do too little, we become complacent or lazy. A balance between the two is having compassion when you fail and being your own best friend when you aren't at your best. Also, by pushing yourself forward past your fears and failure can change the tone in how you feel about yourself, which is what boosting self-worth is all about.

Chapter 13 Relating to Your Family, Friends, and Lovers

Roles

The definitions for codependence can become so broad and convoluted that it seems like almost everybody could be considered codependent in some way shape or form. It gets so diluted that it would be impossible to not fall into one of those categories. Instead look at codependent relationships as a specific type of dysfunction in that someone helps another (read enables) to underachieve, be irresponsible, lack maturity, be addicted, procrastinate, or encourage or hide mental health issues, etc.

Within the dysfunctional family unit we will see the emergence of roles as a way for children to cope with the chaos and drama.

Human beings are funny creatures.

Because we are social animals we will always try to impose a social structure to make sense of our world.

It falls into very predictable patterns.

Keep in mind that the following characteristics may appear in children and adults that are not codependent.

That's not the assumption to make here, otherwise everyone could be considered codependent.

Rather, look at it like this: When someone is exhibiting codependent tendencies the roles we will discuss below will help us identify this person's place in a codependent relationship.

The roles can be based off of their personalities, birth order, or a combination of factors.

We will discuss the following to gain a better understanding of each one and later we will delve into how to treat them in the healing section.

Keep in mind that these roles can change over time and individuals can also hold more than one role simultaneously.

The Addict

Substance abuse is very common in children from dysfunctional homes including alcohol and drug abuse.

The addict in this role lives in a chaotic state and the way they primarily deal with their life is by escaping.

The physical and psychological dependency becomes so ingrained that they identify and make substance abuse a priority in their lives.

They will lie, cheat, and steal to maintain their addiction.

Within the family unit we see the addict take center stage as everything seems to revolve around them.

It does several things, it gives the family something else to focus on rather than their own internal, individual suffering as well as allowing the other dysfunctional roles to flourish.

The Responsible Child or Hero

This is the child that is older than he or she seems.

They take on a parental role at a very early age.

He or she is very responsible and may look great on the outside.

Usually they are great students, athletes, the prom queen.

This is the child parents look to, to say they are doing a fine job in raising their kids.

The family hero can grow up to be controlling and judgmental.

The judgment can extend to others but they are actually judging themselves just as harshly.

This person may have a lot of material success where you see high incomes, the perfect house etc. They are very competitive and driven.

Unfortunately, this stems from insecurity.

This person, the hero, because of his or her rigid and controlling nature and seeming success that you see on the outside will have a very difficult time admitting that there's even a problem.

Now this isn't to say that all high achievers are codependent.

All I am saying is that if there is dysfunction in a family, then this is one of the role that can appear.

Don't confuse this with somebody that becomes a high achiever because they are driven and they want to find success.

Not every driven and successful person is considered codependent.

The Scapegoat

The next role is the child that acts as the scapegoat for all things.

This is the child that gets in trouble for everything.

Trouble seems to find them even if they are not looking.

What is happening is the child is acting out the anger and frustration that the family is ignoring.

This child provides distraction from the real issues.

He or she gets in trouble at school, that is how they get attention.

The only attention they know is the negative type.

This is the child who grows into the teenager who becomes addicted to drugs, becomes pregnant, or gets the girlfriend pregnant.

The scapegoat is usually the most sensitive and that is why there is so much tremendous hurt inside of them.

They cannot put a name on the dysfunction, they just know there is something wrong in the family.

The scapegoats end of growing up to be very cynical and distrustful with a lot of hatred and can be very self-destructive.

It's safe to say there is probably a lot of overlap with the addict.

This person on the other hand is the one that, because their problems are right there on the surface, may seek help first.

They can be the first one to admit that there is a problem and they are not covering anything up.

Everything is right there in the open.

The Mascot

The Mascot

This child is essentially taking responsibility for the emotional well-being of the family.

The class clown.

The funny one.

They want to divert the family's attention from all of the hurt and the anger and the emotional hardships.

A lot of times, this is the person that distracts the attention from the addict.

This person is valued for their kind heart, their ability to stop everything and listen to their friend when they have a problem. Incredibly generous.

Their self-identity is centered on helping others so much so that they do not meet their own needs.

This is the person that cannot receive love, only give it.

It is like they do not take on friendships.

Rather, they become the therapist for their friend.

The mascots tend to get into abusive relationships because they are there to save that person.

You will see them become social workers, therapists, nurses.

In other words, help oriented occupations.

Ruled by guilt and very low self-worth they work hard to never get in arguments with people.

They run their lives by being very agreeable and not wanting to be the bad guy.

This is your quintessential people pleaser.

It is very difficult to overcome this.

It takes a lot of therapy and a lot of self-love for them to come out of this and to understand that it's not their fault, and they are not responsible for everything that goes wrong in other people's lives.

They fit the classic role of the codependent person that is so one-sided and not balanced that they give everything they have and get nothing in return.

The Lost Child

This role tries to disappear.

This is the person that gets lost in fantasy books, plays a lot of video games, watches a lot of movies and TV.

This happens because they do not want to deal with what is going on at home.

They withdraw from from the chaos and deny that there is a problem at all.

So much so that they don't even bother getting angry.

They just withdraw emotionally.

They suffer very low self-esteem and are unable to feel as they get older.

This is the person that does not want to get into a relationship and they have intimacy issues.

These people end up becoming socially isolated.

That is the only way they know how to remain safe and avoid being hurt.

You will see a lot of artists and writers who express themselves through their medium rather than become people that deal with their problems.

At the same time they can hide behind characters or the roles they play.

Again, keep in mind, just because these roles exist does not mean that everyone that is a high achiever is a controller that just because you like to write, doesn't mean you are a lost child.

This is simply a way of identifying roles in a dysfunctional family.

To show that dysfunction is present.

This shows the different roles, if the family is seeking treatment and looking to classify the roles.

They can be tailored to each one as we move into recovery.

Normal Childhood

What if my childhood was normal?

The question comes up a lot, I get it.

You may not have been raised with an alcoholic or an abusive parent.

However, codependency is passed down from generation to generation.

So even if you live in a home where they didn't do these things perhaps your parents experienced it and they are going to end up modeling that behavior to you.

Example: your dad is not an abusive individual towards you, but perhaps he is a workaholic and is never around.

He is a good dad overall and he is trying but he learned this behavior.

He has learned avoidance as a coping mechanism from his family growing up which can lead to issues down the road for his children.

Or maybe, mom was raised in a home where there was a lot of verbal abuse and she is determined to raise her children in an environment that does not support that.

But perhaps that comes off with a repression of feelings.

I am not saying that this is necessarily something terrible but at the same time it is a learned behavior that she cannot control if she is not aware.

The behavior of repressing feelings is now passed on, maybe not the verbal abuse though.

The fact of the matter is we are all human beings, we all have issues, we all do things that are not perfect.

That's what makes us who we are.

There is no such thing as a perfect family.

So a perfect childhood is not possible.

Nobody is perfect.

You would need not just one but two perfect people working together in perfect unison, all the time in order to prevent bad habits and bad imprinting from mom and dad.

It's okay.

The point is we have to understand and recognize it when we do, then the healing can begin.

Discussing Characteristics of Codependency with Jim

"Whoa, this stuff really hits home for me. I mean I can see all of those roles playing out in my family."

"Like what?" I asked.

"Well, my sister got hooked on Vicodin in high school and it seemed like there was always drama with her and we were always doing everything we could to keep her out of trouble and get her into rehab or something."

"How is she doing now?"

"She ended up going to this rehab place in Arizona but from what I hear she's struggling."

"Sorry to hear that."

"Yeah, it sucks for her kids too and I'm seeing the pattern in them as well."

"How so?"

"Well, her oldest is going into seventh grade and seems to be the one taking care of the two younger ones. She gets them off to school and she gets herself ready. My sister is always bragging about her and what a great kid she is. It's true too, she's a great kid. I feel like I'm talking to an adult when we talk. Poor kid's had to grow up too fast though."

"So, the daughter has taken on a care taking role in the family it looks like."

"Yup, that's what I see there too." He said.

"How do you see yourself in what we talked about?"

"You mean what role did I play?"

"Exactly."

"I guess I was the responsible one. I think because I was the oldest. That's why I feel so much for my niece. It's hard watching what she's going through because the pressure she puts on herself is crazy."

"And you can relate, right?"

"Yup, I can. Also, I remember my little brother was always joking around. Heck, he's still like that, he can't seem to be serious about anything. I always wondered why he was like that, now it makes sense."

"It's funny how predictable the roles we adopt are." I said.

"But I don't want to change who I am, I mean I want to keep my personality the way it is you know, I'm not looking to change my outlooks and all that."

"Look at it this way, you aren't looking to change your personality, that's what makes you unique. See it more as you are looking to become your authentic self, one that is true to who you are. Does that make sense?"

He paused lost in thought. "Yeah, that does make sense. A lot of sense actually."

Chapter 14 Making Relationships Work

Often codependency continues to perpetuate due to different reasons. As a codependent person, you must make an effort to understand the reasons that sustain codependency so that you can look for ways to overcome those. You are your own enemy and which is why you struggle to overcome codependency. Sabotaging yourself becomes a constant thing assuming that you don't deserve a good life. Of course, you might have made some mistakes in your past, who doesn't? But not forgiving yourself for past mistakes is not the right decision. You start denying your own strengths and thoughts. There are different ways of self-sabotage, including codependency, aggression, an abusive relationship, denial, and more.

Even after realizing codependency, you will not be able to overcome it because of self-sabotage which can make you feel unworthy which triggers codependency even deeper. To treat codependency, you must believe that you are worthy. You should think of the way a person with self-love would handle the situation that you are in. A person with self-love will not select unhealthy options that might hurt their mind and body.

If you can't love yourself yet, try to fake it for some time and so you will gradually make it true. Self-sabotaging is closing the actual view, which is why you are struggling to see the reality, so when you fake it, you will be able to clear the path slowly, but firmly. If you consider factors like anger, denial, and shame, they perpetuate codependency pretty easily. Hence, you must educate yourself about the factors so you can overcome them.

Anger and denial regarding codependency and your partner

Codependency should not be denied because it is dangerous. If you are denying it, it means you are not ready to accept and change, hence it will continue to remain. Instead of facing the problems in your life, you try harder to save others from facing their problems. The same behavior repeats itself when you deny the fact that you are codependent. Basically, there are different types of denial that you will learn below. Once you understand the types, you can take necessary measures.

Denial Your Partner's Behavior

Denying your partner's behavior is one of the common denials, but you can overcome it. You deny that your partner is addicted and his or her addiction causes a lot of problems in your life. Yet, you are not ready to accept it, which is why codependency perpetuates in your life. This kind of denial is common because codependents have been facing similar situations from their childhood. They might have grown up with parents who are addicts, so it looks normal to them.

The addicts and dependents have gotten used to been taken care of, so they are not ready to take responsibility. And codependents are okay with that because they like to take care of others.

If you deny your partner's behaviors, you must understand that you are walking towards a dangerous destination. You must acknowledge the reality and work accordingly because a relationship can ruin your life if you don't handle it wisely. You must accept the fact that you are not responsible for their behaviors. If they are addicted or relying on you for almost everything, it means you have created the path for it. You should not let anyone hurt you just because you arc codependent. Also, if you deny your partner's behaviors, it doesn't mean that you don't care about them. Of course, you are bothered, but you just don't see the seriousness, or you somehow build up reasons to justify the act. This is the typical behavior of someone who loves their partner, but the love codependents show is extra. They don't make an effort to correct the mistakes; they just ignore them. However ignorance will make things worse.

Denial of Codependency

When you are confronted about codependency, you will deny it, and that's the very first step. You can clearly see that you are codependent, but you are not ready to accept it because you think it's a situation that has made you a codependent. You try to blame the situation and people so that you don't have to discuss codependency. Most codependents don't want to discuss it because they think it will worsen the pain, but it will not. This is one of the reasons why you deny that you are codependent.

Another reason is you are not someone who seeks help from others so if you accept that you are a codependent you'd have to get help from others to treat it. This kind of mentality leads you towards a destructive path. You don't like the fact that someone is taking care of you and being responsible for your behaviors because, for a long time, you've been doing it for others. You don't want others to make you happy as it triggers self-examination at a point. When you are codependent, you can easily avoid self-examination, which is why you turned down help from others.

Denying your true nature, which is codependency, will help you to stay away from professional help and admitting your codependent nature. On the other hand, some codependents don't seek professional help, but they try to treat themselves all alone. They believe that they can figure out the problem by talking to close friends and reading reliable books and articles. But sometimes, this can be dangerous depending on the level of codependency that you have. You may be ashamed to seek help, so you try not to get in touch with professionals. But remember, it is not a wise move.

Denial of Feelings

This is another type of denial which deals with a codependent's feelings. You are not ready to discuss how you feel, and ultimately, you end up denying your feelings. Normally, codependents can easily understand what other people feel and worry about. Plus, codependents spend a lot of time helping others to feel better. But they deny their own feelings which create resentment in their hearts. Codependency gives rise to obsession. When you are obsessed, you get distracted from what's important. Similarly, when you are obsessed with your partner, it will be hard to focus on your feelings because you are worried about your partner's feelings more than yours. If you think about your own feelings and how you have been doing, you will have no solid answers because you have denied your feelings.

Even if you understand your physical pain, you will not understand emotional pain because you are blinded by codependency. Also, growing up, you have not had an environment that lets you share your emotions and feelings. You may have always been the one to listen, not the one to speak. Moreover, you don't understand the reason why you should share your feelings when nobody is there to comfort or listen. Hence you keep denying your feelings from childhood. Actually, feelings serve a purpose even if they are not positive feelings. Through feelings, you understand what you need and don't. If you want to interact with people, you must have the ability to share your feelings. How do feelings help you become better at interacting while overcoming codependency?

- If you are angry, you will be reacting to make changes.

- If you are sad, you will empathize and value human connections.

- If you fear, you will keep dangers at bay even if they are emotional dangers.

- If you are guilty, you will have values that you respect.

- If you feel ashamed, you will not harm others.

- If you feel lonely, you will strengthen your connection with others.

Likewise, every negative feeling serves a purpose. When you deny your own feelings, you won't be able to move forward in life. You will bottle up your feelings for years, and it will always be there in your subconscious mind. When you accumulate pain, you will not be able to overcome it. Instead, constant denial might be your answer. What will happen when you continue to deny your feelings? You will end up depressed, and depression isn't as easy as you think!

Maybe you don't, but most codependents treat resentment as a shield to hide anger. Of course, your past or childhood would have been unpleasant and difficult. Maybe you couldn't express what you feel because nobody bothered to listen but that doesn't mean it will repeat in the future unless you want it to repeat. If you stop denying your feelings, you will be able to lead a healthy and happy life. It is important to talk to your partner and explain how you feel because unlike other healthy relationships, your partner will not understand your feelings. Not because he or she doesn't understand others, but because you have been hiding your feelings from them.

Unresolved feelings will repeat itself. If you overcome denial and anger, you will be able to overcome codependency too. But if you don't, it will perpetuate. And you must learn about the snowball effect to understand sustaining codependency.

The Snowball Effect

This is a concept discussed in psychology to understand something that is not only related to codependency but also many other things in life. We all have dealt with the snowball effect in life. Many times in life, you would have dealt with situations that you thought wouldn't blow up this big, but before you know it, the situation becomes a huge mess. This is metaphorical to a snowball that rolls down the hill and forms something huge. Just like that, the negative feelings and thoughts about yourself can snowball into something huge, and before you know it, there would have been a huge mess. You will not be able to cope with yourself when the snowball gets smashed and creates a huge mess! Certain thoughts make the whole process of opening up to your partner difficult, and some of them are:

- You tend to jump into conclusions without focusing on the evidence.

- You tend to generalize even if you see a single negative thing to support certain activity.

- You often catastrophize because you only think about the worst possible outcome.

- You easily filter the positive things into negative.

- You set strict rules regarding the unrealistic expectation of yours and others.

These negative feelings will increase your anxiety and enhance your negative mindset. When your mind is filtered through these feelings, it can be complicated to see things in the right way. You will not make an effort to change or to motivate yourself to overcome codependency because your mind is filtered that way. If negative emotions and behaviors snowball down the hill, you will not be able to stop it successfully. Hence, you must stop it when it started. Well, stopping the snowball where it started might impossible, but it is not. If you follow a few essential points, you will be able to do it.

- The critical point is to break the chain. Start by challenging a few thoughts and looking at them objectively.

- Write your feelings down or talk to a close friend about it. Also, when talking to them about your feelings if they have something to say, let them because listening is also essential.

- Don't skip your day-to-day activities because when you have a routine, you will be able to distract negative thinking for some time.

- Do engage in mindful activities, exercises, and yoga.

These tips might look simple, but they are not as easy as they sound because consistency and patience are two essential things when you are trying to overcome codependency. If you try to move out of this vicious cycle in one go, you are likely to get hurt. Instead, baby steps will help you overcome codependency without creating a mess. Don't let your mind snowball in the process of healing, so even the process of healing should be done step by step.

Not to forget that a professional can help you out of this vicious circle simply because he or she has the skills and required education. Hence, don't step back if you need professional help.

Chapter 15 Following Your Bliss

If you've been in an abusive relationship before, you know the feeling—constantly worrying that the other shoe will drop. Things might be completely fine within that moment, but you cannot help but feel that things are about to fail somehow. You know that, no matter how good things may be in the moment, that it will not always be that good, and because of that, you cannot help but feel uneasy. This is because, whether you know it consciously or not, you recognize the cycle abuse follows. It goes from a state of idealization to devaluation before finally reaching the discard stage, at which point, the narcissist attempts to hoover you up and start the cycle all over again.

This cycle can be incredibly difficult to break, especially since the narcissist keeps you interested in him and hoping things could get back to the way they were through revisiting the idealization stage, even though it frequently is fleeting and gives way to devaluation quickly. Through each of these stages, the behaviors change, but the one thing that remains consistent is the victim's fear of things escalating and of further abuse.

Idealize

The first step in the cycle is idealization. When you are idealized, you are made to feel as though you are important and desired by the narcissist. You are likely showered with attention and made to believe that you are deeply loved. The narcissist puts you on a pedestal with kind words, making you feel valued, and you eat it up. Especially if you have been starved for this sort of love or affection for any meaningful amount of time by the narcissist during the devalue and discard stages, the idealization stage is like a breath of fresh air after diving a little too deep for your skills and comfort. Just as the lack of oxygen burning your lungs and clouding your mind gets to the point of unbearable, you breach the surface and cannot get enough fresh air, the lack of love in your relationship follows the same pattern. When you arc finally met with the love you have been craving, you feel as though you cannot get enough of it and you want more.

This keeps you hooked to the narcissist, and he understands your fixation on the affection. He then uses it as a weaponized to further idealize you. This is referred to as love bombing. Love bombing is the act of showering a person with praise, kind words, gifts, and other tokens of love or appreciation with the hopes of making the other person hooked on the narcissist. While it sounds as though it would be pleasant, and many people would love to literally be bombed with love, the narcissist weaponizes the love, using it to manipulate his victim, and that is what makes it so insidious. He knows that what he is doing is using the victim's feelings to keep her bound to him, and he does it anyway because it suits him.

For example, imagine that you are in a relationship with a narcissist. You love him with all your heart, but you are also frequently the victim of screaming, being blamed, gaslighting, and isolation from friends and family. The narcissist, after a particularly bad argument, has chosen to shift back to the idealization stage in the cycle. He can sense that you want to leave the relationship, and because of that, he decides to tell you how much he loves and values you. He may leave little notes of affection on your desk before work, or send you flowers or delivery of your favorite food for lunch. He may take you on fancy dates and ask you to go out to dinner with him in hopes of rekindling the love for him that you have been withdrawing from as you have debated leaving. Suddenly, you once again feel like you are the center of his universe, and while you still feel as though you fear you will go back to the way things were when the narcissist abused you last, you are also hopeful that this stage will last forever this time.

Devalue

Unfortunately, no matter how much you may want to cling to the idealization stage, you quickly find the relationship returning to old ways. The narcissist begins to use old tactics again. He stops being so interested in you and likely has begun demeaning you again. His manipulation is ramping up again, and he likely leaves you feeling hurt and confused most of the time. Things are not necessarily bad yet, but the tensions are rising once more.

At this stage, narcissists feel as though they have wasted enough time and energy lavishing their targets with love and affection. Narcissists love shortcuts and the paths of least resistance, and they will take the easiest path to what they want. He feels as though he has sufficiently hooked his target again when he begins the devalue stage. This means he can start to act out the abuse again with what he hopes is little consequence. He begins to belittle his target again, knowing that it will knock her off of the pedestal he placed her atop, and knowing that the result will be the target scrambling to please the narcissist to climb back up. The devaluation stage typically ends with a big blowout of sorts—perhaps the narcissist hurts the victim, or cheats on the victim, or does something else major that is the result of culminating tensions that have steadily been increasing like the pressure within a volcano that is ready to explode at any moment.

Returning to the example begun in the Idealize stage, you may have noticed that your partner has been making snide comments more frequently than he had been. You knew that you felt hurt and upset by the narcissist's choice in words, but when you confronted him, he told you that you were overreacting and that you should let it go and move on. Confused and uncomfortable, you let it go, but you can tell that tensions have gotten worse. Eventually, he hits you and threatens you with serious harm if you were to ever leave him, marking the escalation and explosion of the devaluation stage.

You have been clearly made aware that you do not matter to the narcissist through his words and actions and are now left reeling and attempting to deal with the consequences.

Discard

The discard stage occurs when the narcissist wants to make it clear that you have lost any usefulness you once had. Through abandoning his victim, he makes it clear that the only purpose his victim served was to serve him, and him alone. When he decides that you are no longer serving him to his contentment or that he has found a new toy to pursue instead, he abandons you altogether to get his narcissistic supply fix elsewhere.

At this stage, despite abandoning you, he also gets the satisfaction of knowing that he has hurt you deeper than anyone else ever could simply by leaving you behind and refusing to speak or acknowledge you in any way, shape, or form. You may know that you are better off free of him, but you feel hurt and miss him all the same because you have always loved him despite the abuse he has inflicted.

Repeat

This cycle, once it has been played through, repeats again. The narcissist, when he feels as though you have suffered enough, or he feels as though you may be getting ready to move on from him, will magically reappear, telling you how important you are to him and how leaving you was his biggest mistake. This is called hoovering you back in. Like the hoover vacuum from which the technique draws its name, he attempts to suck you in with sweet words and promises he will never fulfill. He does not care about lying to you because as far as he is concerned, all that matters is his own feelings.

Escaping the Cycle

When you are finally ready to leave the cycle of abuse, you have finally acknowledged that things are not likely to ever change. You finally recognize that in order to better yourself, you have to escape. This is, unfortunately, the most dangerous time for abuse victims, as their abusers rarely are willing to let their victims leave willingly. The narcissist almost definitely will put up a fight to keep you around, but what is important is to recognize that the only way to end the abuse for good is to drop the narcissist for good. Your life will be far happier and healthier if you do.

Leave when it is safe

The first step toward escaping the cycle is escaping the relationship. You need to create a plan to leave and follow through with it. Remember, you must leave when it is safe for you to do so. This is oftentimes when the abuser is at work or attending some other sort of hobby or prior obligation that typically keeps him busy for a regular amount of time away from home. With the abuser preoccupied, you are free to begin moving out. You may be able to request a police escort if you feel unsafe with the idea of leaving while the narcissist is gone, particularly if you fear that he may become irrationally angry and abusive when he realizes you are leaving.

Avoid explaining or downplaying abuse

Once you have escaped, the next step is to make sure you do not say anything or think anything that may devalue what you have been through. Do not minimize the abuse the narcissist put you through—the more specific and honest you are with yourself, the more likely you are to remain firm in your convictions and leave the narcissist for good. However, if you were to try to explain away the abuse, you would likely be more willing to put up with attempts to talk or work out your relationship.

Recognize the cycle—and do not fall for the hoover

By recognizing the cycle of abuse, you regain some of your power. You recognize that the happy periods are little more than oscillations within a cycle, and that cycle will return to violence and abuse again in the future. You know that the abuse will come again, and when you devalue and depersonalize it to that point, you are far more likely to stay away. Just as you would have no qualms avoiding a dog that you knew bit unprovoked, remembering the abuse the narcissist has inflicted can help you stay strong and keep your distance.

Acknowledge your power

No matter what the narcissist may want you to believe, you have power. You have the power to make your own decisions. You have the power to control your own actions and manage your own emotions. You have the power to decide to disengage from the narcissist permanently, and not allow the narcissist to dictate how everything should go. When you acknowledge that you are capable of living by yourself and that you are powerful enough to take care of yourself and your loved ones, you are far more likely to resist the narcissist's hoover attempts.

Reach out to others in moments of weakness

The last step, when breaking the cycle of abuse is to remember to reach out to others. If not some sort of group of friends or family, try seeking out support online or from other people you think or know have been through your situation. Reach out to these people during moments of weakness, when you may be missing the narcissist or wishing things would be different. The plus side to finding people who have been through your situation before you is that they can not only guide and offer advice, they can also show you what your future holds. If you see other people living life happily, you can see that happiness is out there, so long as you put in the effort to attain it.

Chapter 16 The People-Pleaser

On the surface, People-Pleasers just want everyone to be happy. However, People-Pleasers don't believe they're worthy of love unless others love them. To get that love, a People-Pleaser will do everything they can to make people like them. While an independent, empowered person believes they are inherently worthy of love, a People-Pleaser feels that they must earn it by being a social chameleon and changing into whoever the person they're with would like best. With their significant other, a People-Pleaser will put on a happy mask and work very hard to always be what they believe their partner wants, be it "The Breadwinner," "The Domestic Goddess," or "The Pillar of Strength." They'll say "yes" to everything and always defer to their partner's desires because they believe that will make them lovable.

The consequences of being a People-Pleaser are quick and painful. A People-Pleaser is immediately at risk for becoming a doormat to their partner, and if their partner is abusive in any way, the People-Pleaser's life will be miserable. Always prioritizing their partner's needs instead of their own can cause a lot of pain for the People-Pleaser. They won't be able to talk about it with their partner, because a People-Pleaser hates discussing negative emotions, believing it will make their partner stop loving them.

Even if their significant other isn't abusive, it will be hard for them to respect a People-Pleaser, because they'll start to see the People-Pleaser as spineless. They'll get frustrated when the codependent won't be able to make a decision without them, or talk about anything that might be controversial or reveal a difference of opinion. Basically, the partner of a People-Pleaser may get bored with the relationship.

Read on for some signs that you might be a People-Pleaser in your relationship:

• You always go to great lengths to meet your partner's every desire, including canceling plans with other people to do what your partner wants, neglecting work and other hobbies, doing something sexual that makes you uncomfortable, and so on.

• You never say "no," but you feel guilty when you even consider saying no to your partner.

• You're always anxious and apologizing just in case you might have done or said something your partner didn't like.

• You don't feel good about yourself unless your partner is happy with you and giving you compliments, affection, etc.

• You avoid confrontation and have developed systems for skirting around hard topics like finances, politics, and so on.

- When you feel sad, upset, or any other emotion that you feel your partner won't want to see, you shove it down and hide from your partner.

- You put every decision through the "Will this make my partner happy?" filter.

Being The Pleaser With Friends and Coworkers

People-pleasers are very closed off with everyone, including their friends. They tend to not share anything deep about themselves, because they're afraid others won't like what's inside. They'll hide all of their personal struggles, personality traits, and opinions. Relationships with People-Pleasers tend to not go below the surface because of this, meaning even though People-Pleasers know a lot of people, they don't have any true friends of the heart. Additionally, People-Pleasers get manipulated and taken advantage of a lot. Their friends get used to always having the People-Pleaser say "yes" to everything, so whenever they need a favor, they know exactly where to go.

At work, a People-Pleaser can get stressed out a lot. They're always taking on extra work, working really hard, and being taken for granted. They tend to bite off more than they can chew just because someone asked for help. Their own work can suffer because they're trying to juggle everybody else's jobs, too. When it comes to the tough decisions, the People-Pleaser often becomes paralyzed with anxiety knowing that they can't possibly make everybody happy. This can be a big problem when there's deadlines approaching and the boss is breathing down their neck.

Saying "No" to People-Pleasing

Once a person realizes they are lovable and don't have to earn that from anyone, they are free. If you're a People-Pleaser, learning to say "no" and loving yourself are key steps to escaping the codependency of people-pleasing. Your partner's attention and affection doesn't make you lovable - you are lovable on your own. Here are some concrete steps you can take to learn that:

• When your partner asks for a favor, say that you need to think about it. This allows you to think about whether or not it's a good idea to say yes.

• When you're meeting your partner for lunch on your break or you have another commitment coming up, set a time limit, so your partner doesn't monopolize your time.

• Don't give a series of excuses for or apologize for why you can't do something your partner wants. They should respect your decision regardless of the reason.

• Make a list about what you really don't like doing with (or for) your partner versus what you actually do enjoy. Get in touch with your feelings, so you can start having a mind of your own and figuring out what your desires and needs are.

- Start saying "no" to the things on your dislike list, so you can still say "yes" to the things you yourself enjoy.

- When a topic of conversation comes up that usually makes you uncomfortable, be open with your partner about your fears, but don't run away from it. (Note: If your partner is abusive and you avoid topics so you don't get hurt, apply this step to your therapist, friends, family, etc, so they can help you).

- Try to do three things just for you every day.

Coming out of a people-pleasing mindset involves rewiring long-held beliefs about yourself. This may require going to therapy alone and spending time focusing on your own dreams and desires. Here are some thought exercises that can help:

- When you do something just for you, take a moment to analyze your feelings. If you feel guilt, use positive affirmation to tell yourself that it's okay to take care of yourself and your needs.

- Visit a therapist who can help you dig up why you feel selfish and bad when you aren't taking care of someone else's needs.

- If you haven't been in touch with your own feelings and desires in a long time, spend time alone figuring out what you really want out of life and your relationship.

- Work on learning that confrontation and hard conversations are all a part of building a strong, healthy relationship.

- Begin living through a filter of "I should treat myself as lovingly and kindly as I treat others."

- Focus on self-acceptance, self-empowerment, and self-love with the mentality that you cannot give the best of yourself to others unless you are a whole person. This can help you get an idea of the bigger picture and what's at stake for your relationship.

Chapter 17 Being Assertive

Perhaps at this point you are beginning to realize what a big challenge you are facing as you work to put your codependence behind you. You know you need to take charge of your personal boundaries, but you just don't have the tools you need to do it. It can seem very scary, but you can keep going through your fear. The first step to reclaiming your personal boundaries is to learn to be assertive.

What Is Being Assertive?

Being assertive means standing up for yourself in a strong, confident way. When you are assertive, you respect your own position as well as the positions of others. You tell people clearly and honestly how you feel, what you think, and what you need.

Assertiveness is very uncommon on both sides of a codependent relationship. The three other types of communication are passive, aggressive and passive-aggressive. As a partner in a codependent relationship, you likely relied on these other forms of communication to try and get what you wanted.

You communicate passively when you let everything happen as it will. You give little or no input into the conversation. When you do say something, you let others convince you that you are wrong. Your partner dominates the relationship and you are merely along for the ride. People who choose to communicate passively usually fear rejection and/or confrontations.

When you communicate aggressively, you push the other person into doing what you want. You are usually hostile and angry, or you complain loudly and nag your partner to quit his addictive behavior. You insist on having your way, no matter how the other person feels. You use punishments, demands and blaming to assert your dominance. If you are an aggressive communicator, you do not concern yourself with the rights and opinions of your partner.

Often, people who are in a codependent relationship become passive-aggressive. They have their own feelings and opinions about family situations.

But they do not express themselves honestly and openly. Instead, they manipulate or trick their partner to do things the way they want them done.

When you choose to be assertive you decrease misunderstandings. Your partner knows what you want, whether he acts to give it to you or not. You do not try to control your partner. You do take away your partner's power over your life.

How to Be Assertive

Being assertive with your partner for the first time is a big hurdle to cross. Once you have established that you are only going to participate in healthy communications, you change the relationship drastically. And, if you want to stop being codependent, that is exactly what you need to do. Here is a step-by-step guide to help you through those first assertive communications.

Step One: Decide What You Want to Communicate

Deciding what to talk about is not as easy as it sounds. If you are in a codependent relationship, you are more accustomed to talking about your partner and what he needs or needs to do. Instead, focus on your own wants, needs, feelings and opinions. Start by talking about just one thing you want to say about yourself.

Step Two: Speak Clearly and Honestly

When you are in a codependent relationship with an addict, it is easy to think first about saying things in a way your partner will accept. Or, conversely, you might be prone to pushing his buttons and provoking him to lash out at you. This time, just think about expressing your thought or feeling in a way your partner will understand. To speak assertively, you have to be honest and give your partner the message that is in your heart.

Step Three: Let Your Partner Own His Feelings and Responses

Right now you might be thinking about how your partner might react if you speak clearly and honestly about your thoughts and feelings. And the truth is that he might get very upset or withdrawn. He might become angry with you and become verbally abusive. You need to know that before you start being assertive.

Just remember that whatever your partner says, does or seems to think or feel, it is something that belongs to him and him alone. You do not have to feel bad for stating your opinion. You do not have to take abuse for expressing your feelings. You have every right to speak assertively.

Step Four: Respect Your Partner's Rights

One of the hallmarks of healthy and assertive communications is maintaining respect for the other person's rights. An addict can become so wrapped up in his addiction that he allows other people to make his decisions and tell him what is right or wrong for him. You might even feel justified in disrespecting his boundaries because he is in no shape to know what he really wants.

But, you can still practice being assertive regardless of your partner's addiction. Speak up and say what you want or need to say. At the same time, give him the consideration of respecting his thoughts, feelings and opinions.

Learning to be assertive is, for most people, a lifetime task. You can begin with just a few assertive conversations a day, and increase them as you get the hang of it. Eventually, you learn to communicate assertively in every conversation. While there will always be the temptation to resort to being passive, passive-aggressive or aggressive, you have the power to choose assertiveness.

Your life will not always be easier, but it will be healthier. You develop a better sense of self esteem as you speak and act assertively. The reverse is also true: when you feel better about yourself, it is easier to stand up for your own needs and wants. And now we come to the heart of the codependent relationship. You need to improve your self-esteem if you want to break free of codependency and move on with your life.

Chapter 18 The essential dictionary to understanding narcissistic abuse

The world of the narcissist is a complex and different one. It is different from how healthy and sane humans operate. That is why insight on how it feels to be a narcissist will help you learn how to relate. In understanding narcissism and narcissistic personality disorder, this chapter lays the foundation.

What is Narcissism Personality Disorder?

When we talk about narcissism, many people attribute it to people who are full of themselves. While this is true in some ways, narcissism is a personality disorder. It is a severe psychological disorder that revolves around attaching excessive importance to oneself. In fact, narcissism doesn't even have to do with genuine self-love. More appropriately, narcissists are in love with a non-existent image of themselves that exists in their head. They resort to falling in love with this image since it allows them to escape the feeling of insecurity that plagues them deep down. However, it takes a lot of effort to keep up with this false sense of majesty. This is why a narcissistic personality involves a dysfunctional attitude and behavior.

This sense of importance is so excessive, and in no way the same as ordinary people. Those with this disorder are characterized by an inability to think of others, let alone put themselves in other people's shoes. This is coupled with an abnormal need for admiration or acknowledgment.

As a result of their excessive need for admiration, they are usually selfish, manipulative, cocky, arrogant or demanding, etc. This individual exists in almost all social circles you encounter in life. Parents, children, romantic partners, colleagues, etc. all manifest this trait. This leads to serious issues, more severe than someone who attaches a little more importance to themselves.

People with this disorder have this false belief that they are better and superior to all others. This belief, however, has no factual basis. It manifests in the way they interact and relate to others. They are drawn to gifted people or those that can act as a source of fuel to them. People with NPD need this association as a supply for their damaged or fragile self-esteem. This is why they are always on a quest for attention as proof their peers hold them in high esteem.

People with NPD also do not take criticism lightly. Even constructive criticism does not go down well for them. They cannot accept the fact that they are wrong or faulty. As a result, they feel humiliated, injured, or attacked when criticized.

In understanding narcissistic personality disorder, it is vital to know the tenets that define the disorder. A few of these are:

· Authority

· Self-sufficiency (believing your strength and wisdom got you here)

- Exhibitionism

- Superiority

- Vanity

- Entitlement

- Exploitation

These characteristics form the foundation of the disturbing personality found in a narcissist. They have a high affinity for accolades while promoting themselves. This only ends up isolating them more even though deep down, they long for approval and inclusion.

Understanding the Mind of a Narcissist

While many people have an idea of what a narcissist is, we are often clueless about what makes them this way. We often wonder what it feels like to be a narcissist! What makes them tick? What is responsible for the excess importance they attach to themselves?

As we strive to understand the concept of narcissistic personality disorder, it can help shed light on what goes on in their mind. With this, we know the thoughts responsible for their excessive self-importance. In understanding the mind of people with Narcissistic Personality Disorder, we should consider some of their characteristics. They display an exaggerated sense of importance with a need for constant admiration, making them appear entitled. Besides, their self-centeredness is alarming, with an excessive focus on themselves. This makes them dangerously envious with a constant need for reassurance. There is also a strong tendency for narcissists to compare themselves with others. It explains why a narcissist gets the urge to put others down or see themselves as more deserving.

This comparison is a vital tool in maintaining the narcissists exaggerated sense of importance. This comparison takes place in the mind, an offshoot of the critical inner voice. This inner voice is a destructive thought pattern coming from painful and disturbing experiences that form our opinion of ourselves, others, and the world around us. This cruel inner voice fuels the negative conversation going on in our head. For many, this mental dialogue can attack, insult, criticize, and is often self-destructive. It can be hostile and also self-soothing.

For a narcissist, however, what is that critical inner voice saying.

In people with NPD, their critical inner coach concentrates mainly on other people, and how to put them down. This is done to make themselves appear and ultimately feel better. If their boss happens to reward a co-worker, a person with this mindset may think: "He's an opportunist; I could do his job better." Or, they deserved that award more. If a narcissist is interested in dating someone, they are likely to think to be in that person's life would only benefit them, and they would be smart to give in.

Not only are there voices of comparison, but there is also the thought of wanting to be unique, an affinity for attention and admiration.

· "You are clearly better. Do something to get their attention."

· "What a fantastic idea, yours is the only worthwhile one."

· "No one knows what is going on better than you."

· "You deserve to be heard."

To a narcissist, this voice could be due to insecurity that is rooted deeply in their personality. It might also be as a result of an exaggerated sense of importance.

Whatever the case may be, why does a narcissist have to listen to these voices? Will they lose out if they ignore the voices?

Many narcissists have admitted that if they do not feel special, they are not okay. Narcissists operate on both sides of the spectrum. In other words, they are either great or they are nothing. They must be the best at what they do, and everyone must notice it, or it's pointless. This can be traced back to the root of the problem. A distortion in their foundation where they learned that just being themselves or ordinary is not accepted, they have to be the best.

An insight into the mind of a narcissist helps understand their action. Even though they appear strong and confident, deep down, they are weak and predictable. This is why a careful examination of a narcissist's behavior shows that their life follows a pattern, making them less enticing.

Watch out for the following patterns.

They Are Cunning and Have Mastered the Act of Earning People's Trust

They always know just the right words to say, how to captivate people. Remember these people are masters of deception and they know how to seem caring and make you feel important, all in a bid to get close to you.

From a distance, a narcissist is playful, exciting, and lively. It is easy to fall in love with them as they are master seducers with a slew of romantic gestures to shower unsuspecting victims.

Once they have you, it's hard to back out. Your life and relationship will likely be subjected to abuse, trauma, and objectification until it ends. They won't show you their true colors until it's time because they know it will just turn you off. This is why so much effort goes into disguising their real personality.

As you proceed in the relationship, you find yourself reluctant to leave. You have a hard time believing your partner is the problem. This makes you always second guess the things you say or do, which would make anyone go crazy.

They Deceive Without Remorse

Honesty is not in the DNA of a narcissist. They can twist any event to a degree that better suits their selfish needs. Bear in mind that they do not think of their lies, as lies. For example, if they claim you are suffocating them in the relationship, they do not mind telling everyone you know that you are too clingy.

Putting others down means nothing to a narcissist. They target your self-esteem with their insults and abusive words so that your subconscious starts accepting it. With time, you start to look up to them for approval. People on the outside won't see it or them for who they are.

They Have a Deep Sense of Insecurity

Even though narcissists love manipulating and putting others down, true happiness is always far from their grasp. This is because anyone truly happy does not need to bring others down. They are a weak, helpless individual with the consciousness that they lack healthy human interaction.

They may not be able to express it, but they know they are broken. Deep down, this person sees the joy and satisfaction from everyday interactions and relationships elude them. Oh, what a lonely place to be.

Rather than looking inward for growth and self-development, they prefer to depend on others for their source of strength. This ultimately forms a pattern of terrible habits.

How to Recognize a Narcissist

Demands Constant Admiration

The same way a motor vehicle engine needs constant fuel to keep running, a narcissist's sense of superiority needs to a steady supply of recognition. This is different from the occasional compliment that is enough for normal people. Their ego must be constantly fed so they like to be around people they can feed off.

They are fond of having only one-sided relationships in which all that matters are what they can get from it. To make matters worse, they see this attention as a right, and react vehemently should the focus diminish.

Lack of Empathy

You do not have to lack empathy to be a narcissist. However, when someone lacks empathy, alongside a sense of exploitation and entitlement, he or she could be a narcissist. Take note of how they react during the hardship of others. Do they appear insensitive to that person's plight?

Some things that demonstrate a lack of empathy are rudeness, violating your boundaries, taking calls during a conversation, etc. It should be noted that these examples alone do not mean someone is a narcissist.

A Sense of Entitlement

In other words, they act like the universe revolves around them. Not only are they special, but they deserve to be treated better than everyone else. They do not count themselves as subject to rules or boundaries. This is why they feel they can push boundaries without thinking of the consequences.

When people with NPD are wrong, every other person caused it, and the law isn't right. You are supposed to put their needs above yours, for instance, only cook their favorite meal or go out for dinner only when they feel like it, etc. Since all they care about is getting what they want, such a relationship will be one sided. And to them, you are just a pawn in place makc them feel better about themselves.

Exploiting Others

To a narcissist, people in their life are objects or tools to meet their selfish needs. They are not evolved to the point of identifying with the feelings of others. This makes it easy for them to take advantage of others without remorse. They do not care about the effect their behavior has on others. And if you are bold enough to point it out, expect them to lash out in a very negative way.

If you are unlucky to be in a relationship with one, they will always place their needs, feelings, and wants before yours.

Forms a Pattern of Intimidation, Bully and Belittling Others

You are a threat to the narcissist if you are better than them. People who stand up to them and confront them are a threat. In a means to defend themselves, they resort to ridicule and scorn. They have to put others down in a bid to soothe their ego.

This might take the form of insults, bullying, or threatening to force the person to back down. It can also be in a dismissive way to show that the person means nothing to them.

Excessive Feelings of Superiority

Narcissists are fond of putting others down, talking down on people in charge, etc. because deep down, they know they are inferior. To determine if someone is a narcissist, watch how they treat other people such as the gate-man, waiters, bartenders, etc. They hold people of honor in high esteem in a bid to get on their good side while they are critical to people that serve them.

A narcissist never believes he is wrong and must be right in all circumstances. Even if you argue, they will twist and confuse your brain until you succumb.

Be sure to watch out for more than three traits described above before passing someone off as a narcissist. An individual could manifest any of the signs above and not be a narcissist.

Types of Narcissism

More often than not, the word narcissist is commonly used these days. You hear it in the news headlines, day to day conversation, etc. Besides, many people hold the view that a narcissist is someone who thinks excessively of themselves such that others matter a little to them.

When you consider the way narcissism is used, you will think there is a specific pattern that all narcissism conforms. The reality is that narcissism occurs on a spectrum with healthy self-esteem on one end and NPD on the other. As a result, no two narcissists are rarely alike. They come in diverse personality with various modes of revealing their majesty. Besides, the way they affect self-esteem also differs.

Here are the most extreme types of narcissist you might encounter. They could be of any gender (even though, it is common to the male gender.)

Overt Narcissism

They are loud, have a desire to always be heard, in control, and never wrong. They are the most common. They have this feeling of knowing more and better than others. As a result, whether welcomed or not, they will voice their opinion and expect people to agree and go along with them. Things must always go their way and are not ashamed to say it.

They are bullies that believe in painting others bad to look like the good guy. They lash out at others and humiliate them without guilt. They are known to attack people by mocking and belittling them. They are gifted at coining words to downgrade their victims so they feel useless and worthless as humans.

The Covert Narcissist

On the other hand, the covert narcissist puts up a false image in a bid to deceive people. In other words, they will present themselves as kind, loving, and liberal but don't be fooled. They have mastered the art of manipulation to get what they want.

They are usually found in a position of authority such as politicians, teachers, leaders, etc. Since they are masters at deceiving people, they can pretend and put up any front to get what they want.

The Grandiose Narcissist

This is a type we are more familiar with. The grandiose narcissist considers himself as the most successful, more important than anyone else. He derives pleasure in blowing his trumpet and makes himself feel more relevant than necessary. They do this to make you jealous.

The grandiose narcissist feels his duty in the world is to accomplish great things. Truly, if you meet a serious and hardworking type, the achievement could be in sync with the ambitions. As a result, you have no choice but to admire them.

They love having the spotlight on them so any challenge to outshine them will be met with stern disapproval. They will increase their efforts to ensure you don't surpass them.

The Status Antagonist

These types of narcissists believe they are not worthy unless they receive the validations of others. With little or no sense of self, they strive intensely for power, money, and social status. This social status helps keep their self-confidence and intact. They use their achievement as a measuring stick to judge other people.

They are pretty smart in pursuing their goals and passions. As a result, they strive for headship positions: Chairman and Presidents. They only settle for second in command as a last resort.

The Narcissistic Winner

For the narcissistic winner, everything is competition. They have an extreme desire to compete in everything. This is not about competition in sports, academics, and career. It also involves day to day activities like friendship, spirituality, parenting, etc.

These are the type of people that get jealous when good things happen to their friends. Since life, in general, is a competition to them, they believe they are more qualified for the good things of life. They resort to belittling others achievement in a bid to make themselves feel better.

What Causes Narcissism?

We have passed narcissism as stemming from an inferiority complex and low self-esteem. This, most times, is a result of a discrepancy between the idealized self (standards set by others such as parents) and reality. This imbalance triggers a threatening situation which might be real or perceived, causing anxiety. As a result, they resort to defense mechanisms to try and keep the ego intact.

The narcissist employs denial in a bid to defend against the threat (even though that threat is not real) as well as fact distortion and various other techniques familiar to a person like this. Unfortunately, there is little to no research that has been able to pinpoint a definite cause of such a trait. The bright side, however, is that various studies have linked narcissism to genes and child development.

Genes

Narcissistic personality traits, like other disorders, are transferred through the genes due to an abnormality in the cell. As a result, the connection between the brain and behavior can become faulty. This explains why narcissist does not see anything wrong with their behavior, whereas a rational person would.

Environment

Oversensitive Temperament
Watch out for kids who like throwing tantrums to get what they want. They will cry, mope and sulk in a bid to get you to give in to their demands. These sorts of kids are prone to developing traits of narcissism. These kids believe they deserve special treatment which manifests even at an old age.

Too Much Admiration

When you shower a child with excess praise for a special attribute, it will create a distorted view of self. This is because kids relate this to self-importance. In time, they will expect appreciation for things they didn't deserve. The more apparent this admiration becomes, the more they accept that they are.

Excessive Criticism and Excessive Praise

When criticism is high, there is a likelihood of developing low self-esteem. If this continues, it can trigger specific traits of narcissism as a defense mechanism for self-preservation.

On the other hand, when praise and admiration are too much, the child can still develop traits of narcissism. This is because they grew up with the mentality that they are perfect hence should receive special treatment.

Overindulgence

This is not about disciplining your child for every wrongdoing. But if you give them a pass for every misbehavior, they will have no respect for boundaries. They will have no standards and believe they cannot be questioned for their behavior. These sort of children overly think of themselves as they can do whatever it is that pleases them, with no regard for the feelings of others.

Severe Emotional Abuse

Severely reprimanding a child harms their self-esteem. As they strive to learn who they are, they preserve themselves as they a means for survival. To make sense of what is happening to them, they accept that they are the victims in every case. This translates to a lowered sense of morals which robs them of empathy even when they abuse others.

Emulating Manipulative Behaviors from Parents

A kid will likely follow the parent's behavior rather than do what they are told. As a result of this, kids tend to learn the traits of narcissism from watching their parents. Be careful of how you treat wait staff around your children. Treating these people differently from how you treat your children sends the wrong message. Your kid will grow up and think it's okay to treat others like they are beneath them.

Who are the Targets of the Narcissist?

If you were abused by a narcissist, remember it is never your fault. As long as you are a human, you qualify as a potential victim of a narcissist. However, it is helpful to know the types of people that narcissists like targeting. This can help you identify any of these traits that may put you at risk and take steps to protect yourself.

Keep in mind that you do not only have to be weak and pitiful for a narcissist to target you. They enjoy going after strong willed people because of the challenge and joy of bringing a certain person down.

People That Struggle with Low Self-Esteem

Many things can cause someone to develop low self-esteem. It could be a devaluing experience, an abusive upbringing, any type of assault albeit physical or emotional and sexual violation, etc. These similar attributes make someone vulnerable to a narcissist. This is because the experiences over time have reconfigured the brain to accept that a person does not deserve affection, decent kindness or unconditional love. These types of people are alien to the concept of friendship and love.

Narcissist love preying on this particular set of people since they will bend their conscious power to them. This is what makes them an easy target for narcissistic abuse.

People Who Love Rescuing Others

If you have a passion for helping, preserving, curing, restoring, and defending others. You hate injustice and love to fight for a cause. You do not mind a little inconvenience to make things better for someone else, and cruelty to animals may set you off.

This is why you are drawn to the narcissist. Even though you realize you cannot cure that person you gravitate towards each other. You approach the interaction or relationship with the idea of making them feel a little better.

Empathy

Narcissists are easily drawn to empaths because only empaths can supply the steady flow of supply needed to keep them going. Since the narcissist lacks empathy, they are attracted to people that can provide the required amount. Empathic individuals are a great source of emotional fuel for the narcissist. This keeps them feeling good as well as relevant.

It is in an empath's nature to try to see another people's perspective on everything. This is an attribute that fuels the narcissist's behavior, which keeps the abuse going. To a narcissist, they know a simple apology is enough to excuse their wrongdoings. The empathic person, who is also always willing to understand their behavior, pardons their shortcomings. They know that no matter how much they misbehave; it is in the nature of the empath to forgive and let go.

Resilience

In a relationship, the ability to bounce back from abuse, fights, and most issues strengthens the partnership. This is why narcissists are attracted to resilient individuals as they quickly get over abuse. Over the years, resilient individuals have built their tolerance for pain. While this is a helpful attribute to keep one going through the storms of life, it can be used to keep them entangled in an abusive relationship.

Since it is in their nature not to give up easily, abuse is not enough to prompt them to pull the plug on the relationship. Despite detecting threats in their environments, they would rather ignore their instincts and fight for the relationship. To resilience people, they might even judge the love they invest in a relationship by the amount of ill-treatment they can put up with.